FAVORITE BRAND NAME RECIPES™

HOLIDAY RECIPES

Publications International, Ltd.

Pictured on the front cover *(clockwise from top left):* Cheesy Christmas Trees *(page 18),* Veal Chops with Brandied Apricots and Pecans *(page 182),* Country Pecan Pie *(page 274)* and Roast Turkey with Pan Gravy *(page 226).*

Pictured on the back cover *(left to right):* Beef Rib Roast with Mushroom-Bacon Sauce *(page 146),* Crunchy Asparagus *(page 108)* and Cranberry Apple Nut Pie *(page 296).*

ISBN: 978-1-4508-9986-4

Library of Congress Control Number: 2015936260

Manufactured in China.

8 7 6 5 4 3 2 1

Microwave Cooking: Microwave ovens vary in wattage. Use the cooking times as guidelines and check for doneness before adding more time.

Preparation/Cooking Times: Preparation times are based on the approximate amount of time required to assemble the recipe before cooking, baking, chilling or serving. These times include preparation steps such as measuring, chopping and mixing. The fact that some preparations and cooking can be done simultaneously is taken into account. Preparation of optional ingredients and serving suggestions is not included.

Publications International, Ltd.

TABLE OF CONTENTS

JOYOUS STARTERS

Toasted Pesto Rounds

- ¼ cup thinly sliced fresh basil
- ¼ cup grated Parmesan cheese
- 3 tablespoons mayonnaise
- 1 medium clove garlic, minced
- 12 French bread slices, about ¼ inch thick
- 1 tablespoon plus 1 teaspoon chopped fresh tomato
- 1 green onion with top, sliced
  Black pepper

1. Preheat broiler. Combine basil, cheese, mayonnaise and garlic in small bowl; mix well.

2. Arrange bread slices in single layer on ungreased nonstick baking sheet or broiler pan. Broil 6 to 8 inches from heat 30 to 45 seconds or until bread slices are lightly toasted.

3. Turn bread slices over; spread evenly with basil mixture. Broil 1 minute or until lightly browned. Top evenly with tomato and green onion. Season to taste with pepper. Remove to large serving plate.

MAKES 12 SERVINGS

Crabmeat Spread

- 1 package (8 ounces) cream cheese, softened
- ¼ cup cocktail sauce
- 1 package (8 ounces) imitation crabmeat
  Cocktail rye bread and/or assorted crackers

Spread cream cheese evenly on serving plate. Pour cocktail sauce over cream cheese; top with crabmeat. Serve with bread or crackers.

MAKES 1½ CUPS

Toasted Pesto Rounds

Mushrooms Rockefeller

- 18 large mushrooms (about 1 pound)
- 2 slices bacon
- ¼ cup chopped onion
- 1 package (10 ounces) frozen chopped spinach, thawed and squeezed dry
- 1 jar (2 ounces) chopped pimientos, drained
- 1 tablespoon lemon juice
- 1 teaspoon grated lemon peel
- Lemon slices (optional)

1. Lightly spray 13×9-inch baking dish with nonstick cooking spray. Preheat oven to 375°F. Pull entire stem out of each mushroom cap. Cut thin slice from base of each stem; discard. Chop stems.

2. Cook bacon in medium skillet over medium heat until crisp-cooked and tender. Remove bacon with tongs to paper towel-lined plate; set aside. Add mushroom stems and onion to hot drippings in skillet; cook and stir 3 to 5 minutes or until onion is tender. Stir in spinach, pimientos, lemon juice and lemon peel; cook 2 to 3 minutes.

3. Stuff mushroom caps with spinach mixture; place in single layer in prepared baking dish. Crumble bacon; sprinkle over tops of mushrooms. Bake 15 minutes or until heated through.

MAKES 18 APPETIZERS

Zesty Sausage Dip

- 1 pound ODOM'S TENNESSEE PRIDE® Mild Country Sausage, thawed if frozen
- 1 can (10 ounces each) RO*TEL® Original Diced Tomatoes & Green Chilies, undrained
- 1 package (8 ounces each) PHILADELPHIA® Original Cream Cheese, cut into pieces
- Tortilla chips (optional)

1. Heat large skillet over medium-high heat. Add sausage; cook 7 minutes or until crumbled and no longer pink, stirring occasionally. Drain.

2. Add undrained tomatoes and cream cheese; stir until cream cheese melts.

3. Serve warm with tortilla chips, if desired.

MAKES 28 SERVINGS

Mushrooms Rockefeller

Holiday Cheese Tree

   1 package (8 ounces) cream cheese, softened
   2 cups (8 ounces) shredded Cheddar cheese
   3 tablespoons finely chopped red bell pepper
   3 tablespoons finely chopped onion
   1 tablespoon lemon juice
   2 teaspoons Worcestershire sauce
   ¾ cup chopped fresh parsley
     Yellow bell pepper
     Cherry tomatoes, halved
     Lemon peel ribbons
     Pita Cutouts (recipe follows, optional), assorted crackers and/or pretzel sticks

1. Combine cream cheese, Cheddar cheese, red bell pepper, onion, lemon juice and Worcestershire sauce in medium bowl; stir until well blended. Shape into 6-inch-tall cone shape on serving plate. Press parsley evenly onto cheese tree.

2. Using cookie cutters or sharp knife, cut yellow bell pepper into desired shape for tree top. Press tomatoes onto tree and string lemon peel around tree for garland. Prepare and serve with Pita Cutouts, if desired.

MAKES ABOUT 5 CUPS

Pita Cutouts

   6 pita bread rounds, split in half horizontally
     Olive oil
   ¼ cup grated Parmesan cheese

1. Preheat oven to 350°F.

2. Using 3-inch cookie cutters or sharp knife, cut pita rounds into star, tree and bell shapes. Place in single layer on ungreased baking sheet. Lightly brush with oil; sprinkle evenly with Parmesan cheese.

3. Bake 15 to 20 minutes or until crisp. Remove to wire racks; cool completely.

MAKES ABOUT 4 DOZEN

Tip: Use kitchen scissors to easily split pita rounds in half.

Holiday Cheese Tree

Parmesan Polenta

- 4 cups vegetable or chicken broth
- 1 small onion, minced
- 4 cloves garlic, minced
- 1 tablespoon minced fresh rosemary *or* 1 teaspoon dried rosemary
- ½ teaspoon salt
- 1¼ cups yellow cornmeal
- 6 tablespoons grated Parmesan cheese
- 1 tablespoon olive oil, divided

1. Spray 11×7-inch baking pan with nonstick cooking spray. Spray one side of 7-inch-long sheet of waxed paper with cooking spray.

2. Combine broth, onion, garlic, rosemary and salt in medium saucepan; bring to a boil over high heat. Stir in cornmeal. Reduce heat to medium; simmer 30 minutes or until mixture has consistency of thick mashed potatoes. Remove from heat; stir in cheese.

3. Spread polenta evenly in prepared pan; place waxed paper, sprayed side down, on polenta and smooth surface. Cool on wire rack 15 minutes or until firm. Remove waxed paper; cut into six squares and remove from pan.

4. Preheat grill over medium heat. Spray grid with cooking spray. Brush tops of squares with 1½ teaspoons oil. Grill polenta, oil side down on covered grill 6 to 8 minutes or until golden. Brush with remaining 1½ teaspoons oil; turn and grill 6 to 8 minutes or until golden. Serve warm.

MAKES 6 SERVINGS

Sausage Cheese Puffs

- 1 pound BOB EVANS® Original Recipe Roll Sausage
- 2½ cups (10 ounces) shredded sharp Cheddar cheese
- 2 cups biscuit mix
- ½ cup water
- 1 teaspoon baking powder

Preheat oven to 350°F. Combine ingredients in large bowl until blended. Shape into 1-inch balls. Place on lightly greased baking sheets. Bake about 25 minutes or until golden brown. Serve hot. Refrigerate leftovers.

MAKES ABOUT 60 APPETIZERS

Parmesan Polenta

Arugula-Prosciutto Wrapped Breadsticks with Garlic Mustard Sauce

- ½ cup mayonnaise
- 6 tablespoons grated Parmesan cheese
- 2 tablespoons FRENCH'S® Honey Dijon Mustard
- 1 tablespoon chopped fresh basil
- 2 teaspoons minced garlic
- 1 package (4½ ounces) long breadsticks (12 to 16 breadsticks)
- 1⅓ cups FRENCH'S® French Fried Onions, crushed
- ½ pound thinly sliced prosciutto or smoked deli ham
- 1 bunch arugula (about 20 leaves) or green leaf lettuce, washed, drained and stems removed

1. Combine mayonnaise, cheese, mustard, basil and garlic in mixing bowl. Spread half of each breadstick with some of mustard sauce. Roll in French Fried Onions, pressing firmly.

2. Arrange prosciutto slices on flat work surface. Top each slice with leaf of arugula. Place coated end of breadsticks on top; roll up jelly-roll style. Place seam side down on serving platter.

3. Serve wrapped breadsticks with remaining mustard sauce for dipping.

MAKES 16 APPETIZERS

Holiday Appetizer Puffs

- 1 sheet (half of 17¼-ounce package) frozen puff pastry, thawed
- 2 tablespoons olive or vegetable oil

  Toppings: grated Parmesan cheese, sesame seeds, poppy seeds, dried dill weed, dried basil, paprika, drained capers or pimiento-stuffed green olive slices

1. Preheat oven to 425°F.

2. Roll out pastry on lightly floured surface into 13-inch square. Cut out shapes with cookie cutters. (Simple shapes work best.) Place on ungreased baking sheets. Brush cutouts lightly with oil; sprinkle with desired toppings.

3. Bake 6 to 8 minutes or until golden.

MAKES ABOUT 1½ DOZEN

Arugula-Prosciutto Wrapped Breadsticks
with Garlic Mustard Sauce

Turkey Meatballs
in Cranberry-Barbecue Sauce

1   can (16 ounces) jellied cranberry sauce

½   cup barbecue sauce

1   egg white

1   pound ground turkey

1   green onion, sliced

2   teaspoons grated orange peel

1   teaspoon soy sauce

¼   teaspoon black pepper

⅛   teaspoon ground red pepper (optional)

    Nonstick cooking spray

Slow Cooker Directions

1. Combine cranberry sauce and barbecue sauce in slow cooker. Cover; cook on HIGH 20 to 30 minutes or until cranberry sauce is melted and mixture is heated through.

2. Meanwhile, beat egg white in medium bowl. Add turkey, green onion, orange peel, soy sauce, black pepper and ground red pepper, if desired; mix well. Shape into 24 balls.

3. Spray large skillet with cooking spray; heat over medium heat. Add meatballs; cook 8 to 10 minutes or until browned on all sides. Add to slow cooker; stir gently to coat with sauce mixture.

4. Turn slow cooker to LOW. Cover; cook on LOW 3 hours. Serve warm.

MAKES 12 SERVINGS

Honey Nut Brie

¼   cup honey

¼   cup coarsely chopped pecans

1   tablespoon brandy (optional)

1   wheel (14 ounces) Brie cheese (about 5-inch diameter)

    Assorted crackers, tart apple wedges and/or seedless grapes

1. Preheat oven to 500°F. Combine honey, pecans and brandy, if desired, in small bowl. Place cheese on large round ovenproof platter or in 9-inch pie plate.

2. Bake 4 to 5 minutes or until cheese softens. Drizzle honey mixture over top of cheese. Bake 2 to 3 minutes or until topping is heated through. *Do not melt cheese.* Serve with crackers.

MAKES 16 TO 20 SERVINGS

Turkey Meatballs in Cranberry-Barbecue Sauce

Elegant Shrimp Scampi

¼ cup (½ stick) plus 2 tablespoons butter

6 to 8 cloves garlic, minced

1½ pounds large raw shrimp (about 16), peeled and deveined (with tails on)

6 green onions, thinly sliced

¼ cup dry white wine

Juice of 1 lemon (about 2 tablespoons)

¼ cup chopped fresh parsley

Salt and black pepper

Lemon slices and sprigs fresh parsley (optional)

1. Clarify butter by melting it in small saucepan over low heat. *Do not stir.* Skim off the white foam that forms on top. Strain clarified butter through cheesecloth into glass measuring cup to yield ⅓ cup. Discard cheesecloth and milky residue at bottom of pan.

2. Heat clarified butter in large skillet over medium heat. Add garlic; cook and stir 1 to 2 minutes or until softened but not browned.

3. Add shrimp, green onions, wine and lemon juice; cook and stir 3 to 4 minutes or until shrimp turn pink and are firm and opaque. *Do not overcook.*

4. Add chopped parsley and season with salt and pepper just before serving. Garnish each serving with lemon slices and parsley sprigs.

MAKES 8 SERVINGS

Herbed Stuffed Tomatoes

15 cherry tomatoes

½ cup cottage cheese

1 tablespoon thinly sliced green onion

1 teaspoon chopped fresh chervil *or* ¼ teaspoon dried chervil

½ teaspoon snipped fresh dill *or* ⅛ teaspoon dried dill weed

⅛ teaspoon lemon-pepper seasoning

1. Cut thin slice off bottom of each tomato. Scoop out pulp with small spoon; discard pulp. Invert tomatoes onto paper towels to drain.

2. Stir cottage cheese, green onion, chervil, dill and lemon-pepper seasoning in small bowl until just combined. Spoon evenly into tomatoes. Serve immediately or cover and refrigerate up to 8 hours.

MAKES 5 SERVINGS

Elegant Shrimp Scampi

Cheesy Christmas Trees

- ½ cup mayonnaise
- 1 tablespoon dry ranch salad dressing mix
- 1 cup (4 ounces) shredded Cheddar cheese
- ¼ cup grated Parmesan cheese
- 12 slices firm white bread
- ¼ cup red bell pepper strips
- ¼ cup green bell pepper strips

1. Preheat broiler. Combine mayonnaise and salad dressing mix in medium bowl. Add cheeses; mix well.

2. Cut bread slices into Christmas tree shapes with cookie cutter. Spread about 1 tablespoon mayonnaise mixture over each tree. Decorate with bell pepper strips. Place on baking sheet.

3. Broil 4 inches from heat 2 to 3 minutes or until bubbly. Serve warm.

MAKES ABOUT 12 APPETIZERS

RO*TEL® Sweet and Spicy Hot Wings

- PAM® Original No-Stick Cooking Spray
- 2 cans (10 ounces each) RO*TEL® Original Diced Tomatoes & Green Chilies, undrained
- ½ cup sour cream
- 4 tablespoons BLUE BONNET® Spread-tub, melted
- ¼ cup honey
- 32 chicken wing drumettes (about 2 pounds)
- ½ teaspoon salt
- ¼ teaspoon ground black pepper

1. Preheat broiler. Spray broiler pan with cooking spray; set aside.

2. Place 1 can undrained tomatoes in food processor and pulse until finely chopped. Drain chopped tomatoes and combine with sour cream to make dip; set aside. Place second can undrained tomatoes in food processor and pulse until finely chopped. Pour into medium bowl; stir in BLUE BONNET and honey.

3. Place chicken in large shallow baking pan; sprinkle with salt and pepper. Spread half of tomato mixture over wings; turn to coat. Transfer half of wings to broiler pan; broil 10 minutes. Turn wings; spoon half of remaining tomato mixture on wings. Broil 10 minutes or until chicken is no longer pink and tender (180°F). Repeat cooking of remaining wings. Serve with dip.

MAKES 4 SERVINGS

Cheesy Christmas Trees

Savory Pumpkin Hummus

 1 can (15 ounces) solid-pack pumpkin
 3 tablespoons chopped fresh parsley, plus additional for garnish
 3 tablespoons tahini
 3 tablespoons fresh lemon juice
 3 cloves garlic
 1 teaspoon ground cumin
 ½ teaspoon salt
 ⅛ teaspoon black pepper
 ⅛ teaspoon ground red pepper, plus additional for garnish
    Assorted vegetable sticks

1. Combine pumpkin, 3 tablespoons parsley, tahini, lemon juice, garlic, cumin, salt, black pepper and ⅛ teaspoon ground red pepper in food processor or blender; process until smooth. Cover and refrigerate at least 2 hours to allow flavors to blend.

2. Sprinkle with additional ground red pepper, if desired. Garnish with additional parsley. Serve with assorted vegetable sticks.

MAKES 1½ CUPS

Festive Franks

 1 can (8 ounces) crescent roll dough
 5½ teaspoons barbecue sauce, plus additional for serving
 ⅓ cup finely shredded sharp Cheddar cheese
 8 hot dogs
 ¼ teaspoon poppy seeds (optional)

1. Preheat oven to 350°F. Spray large baking sheet with nonstick cooking spray; set aside.

2. Unroll dough and separate into 8 triangles. Cut each triangle in half lengthwise to make 2 triangles. Lightly spread barbecue sauce over each triangle. Sprinkle with cheese.

3. Cut each hot dog in half. Place one hot dog piece at large end of one dough triangle. Roll up jelly-roll style from wide end. Place point-side down on prepared baking sheet. Sprinkle with poppy seeds, if desired. Repeat with remaining dough and hot dog pieces.

4. Bake 13 minutes or until golden brown. Cool 1 to 2 minutes on baking sheet. Serve with additional barbecue sauce for dipping.

MAKES 16 SERVINGS

Savory Pumpkin Hummus

Mini Merry Meatballs

½   pound ground beef Brisket
¼   pound ground beef Ribeye Steak Boneless
¼   pound Ground Beef (80% lean)
1   cup seasoned stuffing mix
1   egg, beaten
3   tablespoons water
1   teaspoon minced garlic
¼   teaspoon salt
⅛   teaspoon pepper

Cranberry Barbecue Sauce
2   teaspoons vegetable oil
½   cup chopped white onion
1   tablespoon minced garlic
2½ cups fresh cranberries
½   cup orange juice
½   cup water
⅓   cup ketchup
¼   cup light brown sugar
2   tablespoons cider vinegar
2   tablespoons molasses
½   teaspoon ground red pepper
    Salt

1. Preheat oven to 400°F. Combine Brisket, Ribeye, Ground Beef, stuffing mix, egg, water, garlic, salt and pepper in large bowl, mixing lightly but thoroughly. Shape into twenty-four 1½-inch meatballs. Place on rack in broiler pan that has been sprayed with cooking spray. Bake in 400°F oven 13 to 15 minutes until 160°F.

2. Meanwhile, prepare Cranberry Barbecue Sauce. Heat oil in medium saucepan over medium heat. Add onion and garlic; cook and stir 2 to 3 minutes or until tender, but not brown. Add remaining ingredients, stirring to combine. Bring to boil; reduce heat and simmer 20 minutes or until cranberries burst and mixture has reduced to thick consistency, stirring occasionally. Remove from heat; cool slightly. Transfer mixture to blender container. Cover, allowing steam to escape. Process until smooth. Season with salt, as desired.

3. Serve meatballs with Cranberry Barbecue Sauce.

MAKES 24 MEATBALLS

Favorite Recipe Courtesy **The Beef Checkoff**

Nutty Bacon Cheese Ball

  1   package (8 ounces) cream cheese, softened

  ½   cup milk

  2   cups (8 ounces) shredded sharp Cheddar cheese

  2   cups (8 ounces) shredded Monterey Jack cheese

  ¼   cup crumbled blue cheese

 10   slices bacon, cooked, crumbled and divided

  ¾   cup finely chopped pecans, divided

  ¼   cup finely minced green onions (white parts only)

  1   jar (2 ounces) diced pimientos, drained

      Salt and black pepper

  ¼   cup minced fresh parsley

  1   tablespoon poppy seeds

1. Beat cream cheese and milk in large bowl with electric mixer at low speed until blended. Add cheeses; beat at medium speed until well mixed. Add half of bacon, half of pecans, green onions and pimientos; beat at medium speed until well mixed. Season with salt and pepper. Remove half of mixture to large piece of plastic wrap. Shape into ball; wrap tightly. Repeat with remaining mixture. Refrigerate at least 2 hours or until chilled.

2. Combine remaining bacon, pecans, parsley and poppy seeds in pie plate. Remove plastic wrap from chilled cheese balls. Roll each in bacon mixture until well coated. Wrap ball tightly in plastic wrap; refrigerate up to 24 hours.

MAKES ABOUT 24 SERVINGS

Nicole's Cheddar Crisps

1¾ cups all-purpose flour

½ cup yellow cornmeal

¾ teaspoon sugar

¾ teaspoon salt

½ teaspoon baking soda

½ cup (1 stick) butter

1½ cups (6 ounces) shredded sharp Cheddar cheese

½ cup cold water

2 tablespoons white vinegar

Coarsely ground black pepper

1. Combine flour, cornmeal, sugar, salt and baking soda in large bowl. Cut in butter with pastry blender or two knives until mixture resembles coarse crumbs. Stir in cheese, water and vinegar with fork until mixture forms soft dough. Cover dough; refrigerate 1 hour or freeze 30 minutes until firm.*

2. Preheat oven to 375°F. Grease two medium baking sheets. Divide dough into four pieces. Roll each piece into paper-thin circle, about 13 inches in diameter, on floured surface. Sprinkle with pepper; press pepper firmly into dough.

3. Cut each circle into eight wedges; place on prepared baking sheets. Bake 10 minutes or until crisp. Store in airtight container up to three days.

*To prepare frozen dough, thaw in the refrigerator before proceeding as directed.

MAKES 32 CRISPS

Nicole's Cheddar Crisps

Beefy Stuffed Mushrooms

1 pound ground beef
2 teaspoons prepared horseradish
1 teaspoon chopped fresh chives
1 clove garlic, minced
¼ teaspoon black pepper
18 large mushrooms
⅔ cup dry white wine

1. Preheat oven to 350°F. Combine beef, horseradish, chives, garlic and pepper in medium bowl; mix well.

2. Remove stems from mushrooms; fill caps with beef mixture. Place stuffed mushrooms in shallow baking dish; pour wine over mushrooms.

3. Bake 20 minutes or until meat is browned and cooked through.

MAKES 1½ DOZEN

Cheese Pinecones

2 cups (8 ounces) shredded Swiss cheese
½ cup (1 stick) butter, softened
3 tablespoons milk
2 tablespoons dry sherry or milk
⅛ teaspoon ground red pepper
1 cup finely chopped blanched almonds
¾ cup slivered blanched almonds
¾ cup sliced almonds
½ cup whole almonds
Sprigs fresh rosemary (optional)
Assorted crackers

1. Beat cheese, butter, milk, sherry and ground red pepper in medium bowl with electric mixer at low speed until smooth; stir in chopped almonds.

2. Divide mixture into three equal portions; shape each into tapered oval to resemble pinecone. Insert slivered, sliced or whole almonds into each cone. Cover; refrigerate 2 to 3 hours or until firm.

3. Arrange cheeseballs on wooden board or large serving plate. Garnish with rosemary. Serve with assorted crackers.

MAKES 12 TO 16 SERVINGS

Beefy Stuffed Mushrooms

Onion, Cheese and Tomato Tart

Parmesan-Pepper Dough (recipe follows)
1   tablespoon butter
1   medium onion, thinly sliced
1   cup (4 ounces) shredded Swiss cheese
2   to 3 ripe tomatoes, sliced
    Black pepper
2   tablespoons chopped fresh chives

1. Prepare Parmesan-Pepper Dough. Melt butter in large skillet over medium heat. Add onion; cook and stir 20 minutes or until tender.

2. Spread onion over prepared dough. Sprinkle with cheese. Let rise in warm place 20 to 30 minutes or until edges are puffy.

3. Preheat oven to 400°F. Top dough with tomatoes. Sprinkle with pepper. Bake 25 minutes or until edges are deep golden and cheese is melted. Let cool 10 minutes. Transfer to serving platter. Sprinkle with chives. Cut into wedges before serving.

MAKES 6 TO 8 SERVINGS

Parmesan-Pepper Dough

1   package (¼ ounce) active dry yeast
1   tablespoon sugar
⅔   cup warm water (105° to 115°F)
2   cups all-purpose flour, divided
¼   cup grated Parmesan cheese
1   teaspoon salt
½   teaspoon black pepper
1   tablespoon olive oil

1. Sprinkle yeast and sugar over warm water in small bowl; stir until yeast is dissolved. Let stand 5 minutes or until mixture is bubbly.

2. Combine 1¾ cups flour, cheese, salt and pepper in large bowl. Pour yeast mixture and oil over flour mixture and stir until mixture clings together.

3. Turn out dough onto lightly floured surface. Knead 8 to 10 minutes or until smooth and elastic, adding remaining ¼ cup flour if necessary. Shape dough into a ball; place in large greased bowl. Turn dough so that top is greased. Cover with towel; let rise in warm place 1 hour or until doubled in bulk.

4. Punch down dough. Knead on lightly floured surface 1 minute or until smooth. Flatten into a disc. Roll dough to make 11-inch round. Press into bottom and up side of buttered 9- or 10-inch tart pan with removable bottom.

Onion, Cheese and Tomato Tart

Angelic Deviled Eggs

6 eggs
¼ cup cottage cheese
3 tablespoons ranch dressing
2 teaspoons Dijon mustard
2 tablespoons minced fresh chives or dill
1 tablespoon diced well-drained pimientos or roasted red pepper
Sprigs fresh dill (optional)

1. Place eggs in medium saucepan; add enough water to cover by 1 inch. Cover and bring to a boil over high heat. Remove from heat; let stand 15 minutes. Drain. Add cold water to eggs in saucepan; let stand until eggs are cool. Drain and peel.

2. Cut eggs in half lengthwise. Remove yolks, reserving 3 yolk halves. Discard remaining yolks or reserve for another use. Place egg whites, cut sides up, on serving plate; cover with plastic wrap. Refrigerate while preparing filling.

3. Combine cottage cheese, dressing, mustard and reserved yolk halves in food processor or blender; process until smooth. Transfer cheese mixture to small bowl; stir in chives and pimientos. Spoon into egg whites. Cover and refrigerate at least 1 hour. Garnish with dill sprigs.

MAKES 12 SERVINGS

Bacon & Cheese Dip

2 packages (8 ounces each) cream cheese, softened and cut into cubes
4 cups (16 ounces) shredded sharp Cheddar cheese
1 cup evaporated milk
2 tablespoons yellow mustard
1 tablespoon chopped onion
2 teaspoons Worcestershire sauce
½ teaspoon salt
1 pound bacon, crisp-cooked and crumbled
Assorted cut-up vegetables or crusty French bread slices

Slow Cooker Directions

Combine cream cheese, Cheddar cheese, evaporated milk, mustard, onion, Worcestershire sauce and salt in slow cooker. Cover; cook on LOW 1 hour or until cheese melts, stirring occasionally. Stir in bacon. Serve with vegetables or bread slices.

MAKES ABOUT 4 CUPS

Angelic Deviled Eggs

Spinach Cheese Bundles

1 package (6½ ounces) garlic-and-herb spreadable cheese
½ cup packed chopped spinach
¼ teaspoon black pepper
1 package (about 17 ounces) frozen puff pastry, thawed
Sweet and sour sauce (optional)

1. Preheat oven to 400°F. Combine cheese, spinach and pepper in small bowl; mix well.

2. Roll out each sheet of puff pastry into 12-inch square on lightly floured surface. Cut each square into 16 (3-inch) squares. Place about 1 teaspoon cheese mixture in center of each square. Brush edges of squares with water. Bring edges together over filling; twist tightly to seal. Fan out corners of puff pastry.

3. Place bundles 2 inches apart on ungreased baking sheets. Bake 13 minutes or until golden brown. Serve warm with sweet and sour sauce, if desired.

MAKES 32 BUNDLES

Chicken and Rice Puffs

1 box frozen puff pastry shells, thawed
1 package (about 6 ounces) long grain and wild rice mix
2 cups cubed cooked chicken
½ can (10¾ ounces) condensed cream of chicken soup, undiluted
⅓ cup chopped slivered almonds, toasted
⅓ cup diced celery
⅓ cup diced red bell pepper
⅓ cup chopped fresh parsley
¼ cup diced onion
¼ cup chicken broth or dry white wine
2 tablespoons half-and-half (optional)

1. Bake pastry shells according to package directions. Keep warm.

2. Prepare rice according to package directions.

3. Add remaining ingredients to rice; mix well. Cook over medium heat 4 to 5 minutes or until bubbly and heated through. Fill pastry shells with rice mixture. Serve immediately.

MAKES 6 SERVINGS

Tip: This is a delicious way to use leftover chicken or turkey.

Spinach Cheese Bundles

Maple-Glazed Meatballs

2 packages (about 16 ounces each) frozen fully cooked meatballs, partially thawed and separated

1 can (20 ounces) pineapple chunks in juice, drained

1½ cups ketchup

1 cup maple syrup or maple-flavored syrup

⅓ cup soy sauce

1 tablespoon quick-cooking tapioca

1 teaspoon dry mustard

½ teaspoon ground allspice

Slow Cooker Directions

1. Combine meatballs, pineapple chunks, ketchup, maple syrup, soy sauce, tapioca, mustard and allspice in slow cooker.

2. Cover; cook on LOW 5 to 6 hours. Stir before serving.

MAKES ABOUT 48 MEATBALLS

Mini Asparagus Quiches

8 stalks asparagus

3 eggs

¼ teaspoon salt

¼ teaspoon black pepper

1 unbaked 9-inch pie crust

1. Preheat oven to 300°F. Spray 20 mini (1¾-inch) muffin cups with nonstick cooking spray.

2. Trim asparagus; thinly slice on the diagonal or coarsely chop enough to make ½ cup. Bring 3 cups water to a boil in medium saucepan. Add asparagus; cook 2 minutes over medium heat. Drain in colander; rinse under cold water.

3. Whisk eggs, salt and pepper in medium bowl; stir in asparagus.

4. Roll out pie crust dough to 13-inch circle. Cut out circles using 3-inch round biscuit cutter. Gather and reroll scraps to make 20 circles. Press circles into prepared muffin cups. Fill cups with egg mixture.

5. Bake 30 minutes or until tops are lightly browned and toothpick inserted into centers comes out clean.

MAKES 20 MINI QUICHES

Maple-Glazed Meatballs

Grilled Lobster, Shrimp and Calamari Seviche

- ¾ cup orange juice
- ⅓ cup lime juice
- 2 jalapeño peppers,* seeded and minced
- 2 tablespoons chopped fresh cilantro, chives or green onion tops
- 2 tablespoons tequila
- 1 teaspoon honey
- 1 teaspoon ground cumin
- 1 teaspoon olive oil
- 10 squid, cleaned and cut into rings and tentacles
- ½ pound medium raw shrimp, peeled and deveined
- 2 lobster tails (8 ounces each), meat removed and shells discarded

*Jalapeño peppers can sting and irritate the skin, so wear rubber gloves when handling peppers and do not touch your eyes.

1. Combine orange juice, lime juice, jalapeño peppers, cilantro, tequila and honey in medium bowl. Measure ¼ cup marinade into small bowl; stir in cumin and oil. Reserve. Refrigerate remaining marinade.

2. Prepare grill for direct cooking over medium-high heat.

3. Bring 1 quart water to a boil in large saucepan over high heat. Add squid; cook 30 seconds or until opaque. Drain. Rinse under cold water; drain. Add squid to refrigerated marinade.

4. Thread shrimp onto metal skewers. Brush shrimp and lobster with reserved ¼ cup marinade.

5. Place shrimp on grid. Grill shrimp, uncovered, 2 to 3 minutes per side or until pink and opaque. Remove shrimp from skewers; add to squid. Place lobster on grid. Grill 5 minutes per side or until meat turns opaque and is cooked through. Slice lobster meat into ¼-inch-thick slices; add to squid and shrimp mixture. Refrigerate at least 2 hours or overnight.

MAKES 6 APPETIZERS

Grilled Lobster, Shrimp and Calamari Seviche

Goat Cheese Crostini
with Sweet Onion Jam

1 tablespoon olive oil

2 medium yellow onions, thinly sliced

¾ cup dry red wine

¼ cup water

2 tablespoons packed brown sugar

1 tablespoon balsamic vinegar

1 teaspoon salt

¼ teaspoon black pepper

2 ounces soft goat cheese

2 ounces cream cheese, softened

1 teaspoon chopped fresh thyme, plus additional for garnish

1 loaf (16 ounces) French bread, cut into 24 slices (about 1 inch thick), lightly toasted

1. Heat oil in large skillet over medium heat. Add onions; cook and stir 10 minutes. Add wine, water, brown sugar, vinegar, salt and pepper; bring to a simmer. Reduce heat to low; cook, uncovered, 15 to 20 minutes or until all liquid is absorbed. (If mixture appears dry, stir in a few tablespoons of additional water.) Cool 30 minutes or cover and refrigerate until ready to use.

2. Meanwhile, stir goat cheese, cream cheese and 1 teaspoon thyme in small bowl until well blended.

3. Spread ½ teaspoon goat cheese mixture on each slice of bread. Top with 1 teaspoon onion jam. Garnish with additional thyme.

MAKES 24 CROSTINI

Famous Queso Dip

1 can (10 ounces each) RO*TEL® Original Diced Tomatoes & Green Chilies, undrained

1 package (16 ounces each) VELVEETA®, cut into ½-inch cubes

1. Combine undrained tomatoes and VELVEETA in medium saucepan.

2. Cook over medium heat 5 minutes or until VELVEETA is melted completely and mixture is blended, stirring frequently.

3. Serve warm as a dip with tortilla chips, crackers or cut-up fresh vegetables.

MAKES 2½ CUPS

Goat Cheese Crostini with Sweet Onion Jam

Mini Pimiento Cheese Pumpkins

½   package (4 ounces) cream cheese, softened
1   cup (4 ounces) finely shredded sharp Cheddar cheese
1   cup (4 ounces) finely shredded Monterey Jack cheese
¼   cup mayonnaise
1   jar (2 ounces) pimientos, plus juice as needed
1   teaspoon grated onion
¼   teaspoon salt
⅛   teaspoon black pepper
⅛   teaspoon garlic powder
¾   cup finely chopped smoked almonds
12   mini pretzel sticks
12   fresh parsley leaves
    Assorted crackers

1. Beat cream cheese in medium bowl with electric mixer on medium speed until light and fluffy. Add cheeses; beat until combined. Add mayonnaise, pimientos, onion, salt, pepper and garlic powder; beat until well blended. Beat in pimento juice, if desired. Refrigerate until firm.

2. Shape mixture into equal-size balls. Immediately roll in almonds. Use pretzel to make small dimple on top of ball to form pumpkin shape; insert pretzel in center of dimple for stem. Press parsley leaf around stem and into cheese ball. Serve with crackers.

MAKES 6 TO 8 SERVINGS

tip   Pulse almonds in a food processor or blender to make chopping the nuts easier.

Mini Pimiento Cheese Pumpkins

SPLENDID
SOUPS & SALADS

Split Pea Soup

1 package (16 ounces) dried green or yellow split peas

7 cups water

1 pound smoked ham hocks *or* 4 ounces smoked sausage links, sliced and quartered

2 carrots, chopped

1 onion, chopped

¾ teaspoon salt

½ teaspoon dried basil

¼ teaspoon dried oregano

¼ teaspoon black pepper

1. Rinse peas thoroughly in colander under cold running water; discard any debris or blemished peas.

2. Combine peas, water, ham hocks, carrots, onion, salt, basil, oregano and pepper in Dutch oven; bring to a boil over high heat. Reduce heat to medium-low; simmer 1 hour 15 minutes or until tender, stirring occasionally. Stir frequently near end of cooking to keep soup from scorching.

3. Remove ham hocks; let stand until cool enough to handle. Remove ham from hocks; chop. Discard bones.

4. Place 3 cups soup in blender or food processor; blend until smooth. Return to Dutch oven; stir in ham. If soup is too thick, add water until desired consistency is reached and cook just until heated through.

MAKES 6 SERVINGS

Tip: To purée soup, carefully pour the hot mixture into the blender. Cover with the lid, removing the center cap, then cover the hole with a towel. Start blending at low speed and gradually increase to high speed, blending to desired consistency.

Split Pea Soup

Orange Poppy Seed Salad

Honey & Poppy Seed Dressing (recipe follows)
Lettuce leaves
2 oranges, peeled and sliced crosswise
1 small red onion, sliced and separated into rings
½ small jicama, cut into ½-inch strips

1. Prepare Honey & Poppy Seed Dressing; set aside.

2. Arrange lettuce leaves on serving plates; top with oranges, onion and jicama. Serve with dressing.

MAKES 4 SERVINGS

Honey & Poppy Seed Dressing

½ cup mayonnaise
¼ cup sour cream or plain yogurt
2 tablespoons honey
1 tablespoon lemon juice
1 teaspoon poppy seeds

Whisk mayonnaise, sour cream, honey, lemon juice and poppy seeds in small bowl until well blended. (Dressing may be thinned with a few tablespoons milk, if desired.)

MAKES ¾ CUP

Orange Poppy Seed Salad

Baked Potato Soup

3   cans (10¾ ounces each) condensed cream of mushroom soup
4   cups milk
3   cups diced peeled baked potatoes
½   cup cooked crumbled bacon
1   tablespoon fresh thyme leaves *or* 1 teaspoon dried thyme leaves
    Sour cream and shredded Cheddar cheese
1½ cups FRENCH'S® French Fried Onions

1. Combine soup and milk in large saucepan until blended. Stir in potatoes, bacon and thyme. Cook over medium heat about 10 to 15 minutes or until heated through, stirring frequently. Season to taste with salt and pepper.

2. Ladle soup into serving bowls. Top each serving with sour cream, cheese and 3 tablespoons French Fried Onions.

MAKES 8 SERVINGS

Caramelized Apple & Onion Salad

¼   cup I CAN'T BELIEVE IT'S NOT BUTTER!® Spread
2   large Granny Smith or other tart apples, peeled, cored and thinly sliced
1   large onion, sliced
6   cups mixed salad greens or mesclun
½   cup WISH-BONE® Balsamic Vinaigrette Dressing
½   cup toasted chopped walnuts or pecans (optional)

In 12-inch skillet, melt I Can't Believe It's Not Butter!® Spread over medium-high heat and cook apple and onion, stirring occasionally, 4 minutes or until tender. Reduce heat to medium and cook uncovered, stirring occasionally, 20 minutes or until apple and onion are golden brown. Serve warm apple mixture over greens. Drizzle with dressing and garnish with walnuts.

MAKES 6 SERVINGS

Baked Potato Soup

Warm Steak Salad with Mustard Dressing

Mustard Dressing (recipe follows)
1 beef flank steak (about 1¼ pounds)
Salt and black pepper
¼ pound sugar snap peas or snow peas
Lettuce leaves
1 medium red onion, sliced and separated into rings
1 pint cherry tomatoes, halved

1. Preheat broiler. Position oven rack about 4 inches from heat source.

2. Prepare Mustard Dressing; set aside.

3. Place steak on rack of broiler pan. Broil 13 to 18 minutes for medium-rare to medium or until desired doneness, turning once. Season with salt and pepper.

4. Meanwhile, bring lightly salted water to a boil in medium saucepan. Add peas; cook 2 minutes. Drain.

5. Place steak on cutting board. Cut across the grain into thin slices.

6. Line serving platter with lettuce. Arrange steak slices in center of platter. Surround with onion rings, snow peas and cherry tomatoes. Serve with dressing.

MAKES 4 SERVINGS

Mustard Dressing

¾ cup olive oil
3 tablespoons seasoned rice vinegar
1 tablespoon balsamic vinegar
1 tablespoon Dijon mustard*
¼ teaspoon dried thyme
Salt and black pepper

Substitute coarse-grind mustard for Dijon mustard.

Whisk oil, vinegars, mustard and thyme in small bowl until well blended. Season with salt and pepper.

MAKES ABOUT 1 CUP

Warm Steak Salad with Mustard Dressing

Italian Fish Soup

4 ounces fresh halibut or haddock steak, 1 inch thick
1 cup meatless pasta sauce
¾ cup chicken broth
¾ cup water
1 teaspoon Italian seasoning
¾ cup uncooked small pasta shells
1½ cups frozen vegetable blend, such as broccoli, carrots and water chestnuts or broccoli, carrots and cauliflower

1. Remove skin from fish. Cut fish into 1-inch pieces. Cover and refrigerate until needed.

2. Combine pasta sauce, broth, water and Italian seasoning in medium saucepan; bring to a boil. Stir in pasta. Return to a boil. Reduce heat and simmer, covered, 5 minutes.

3. Stir in fish and frozen vegetables. Return to a boil. Reduce heat and simmer, covered, 4 to 5 minutes or until fish flakes easily when tested with fork and pasta is tender.

MAKES 2 SERVINGS

Mixed Greens with Raspberry Vinaigrette

½ cup walnuts, toasted*
⅓ cup vegetable oil
2½ tablespoons raspberry vinegar
1 tablespoon chopped shallot
½ teaspoon salt
½ teaspoon sugar
2 cups washed and torn romaine lettuce
2 cups washed and torn spinach
2 cups washed and torn red leaf lettuce
1 cup halved red seedless grapes

*To toast walnuts, spread in single layer in heavy skillet. Cook over medium heat 1 to 2 minutes or until nuts are lightly browned, stirring frequently.

1. Coarsely chop walnuts; set aside. Whisk oil, vinegar, shallot, salt and sugar in small bowl until well blended. Cover; refrigerate up to one week.

2. Combine romaine, spinach, red leaf lettuce, grapes and walnuts in large bowl; toss to blend. Add dressing just before serving; toss well to coat.

MAKES 6 TO 8 SERVINGS

Italian Fish Soup

Roasted Sweet Potato and Apple Salad

2 large sweet potatoes, peeled and cubed

Nonstick cooking spray

½ teaspoon salt, divided

¼ teaspoon black pepper

3 tablespoons apple juice cocktail

1 tablespoon olive oil

1 tablespoon balsamic vinegar

1 tablespoon Dijon mustard

1 tablespoon honey

2 teaspoons snipped fresh chives

1 medium Gala apple, cored and chopped (about 1 cup)

½ cup finely chopped celery

¼ cup thinly sliced red onion

Lettuce leaves

1. Preheat oven to 450°F. Arrange sweet potatoes in single layer on baking sheet. Spray with cooking spray; season with ¼ teaspoon salt and pepper. Roast 20 to 25 minutes or until potatoes are tender, stirring halfway through. Cool completely.

2. Meanwhile, whisk apple juice cocktail, oil, vinegar, mustard, honey, chives and remaining ¼ teaspoon salt in small bowl until smooth and well blended.

3. Combine sweet potatoes, apple, celery and onion in medium bowl; toss to combine. Drizzle with dressing; gently toss to coat.

4. Arrange lettuce leaves on four serving plates. Top evenly with sweet potato mixture.

MAKES 4 SERVINGS

Navy Bean & Ham Soup

6 cups water

5 cups dried navy beans, soaked overnight, rinsed and drained

1 pound ham, cubed

1 can (about 15 ounces) corn, drained

1 can (about 4 ounces) diced mild green chiles, drained

1 onion, chopped

Salt and black pepper

Slow Cooker Directions

Place water, beans, ham, corn, chiles, onion, salt and pepper in slow cooker. Cover; cook on LOW 8 to 10 hours or until beans are softened.

MAKES 6 SERVINGS

Roasted Sweet Potato and Apple Salad

Italian Wedding Soup

- 1   pound lean ground beef
- 1   egg *or* 2 egg whites
- ½   cup fresh bread crumbs
- 3   tablespoons grated Parmesan cheese
- 2   tablespoons grated onions
- ¼   teaspoon ground black pepper
- 12   cups SWANSON® Chicken Broth (Regular, Natural Goodness® *or* Certified Organic)
- 1   teaspoon onion powder
- 1   teaspoon garlic powder
- 1   teaspoon celery salt
- ⅔   cup orzo pasta (rice-shaped pasta)
- 2   cups thinly sliced escarole
-    Grated Parmesan cheese

1. Thoroughly mix the beef, egg, bread crumbs, cheese, onions and pepper. Shape **firmly** into ½-inch balls.

2. Heat the broth, onion powder, garlic powder and celery salt in a 6-quart saucepot over medium-high heat to a boil. Stir the meatballs into the saucepot. Reduce the heat to low and cook for 10 minutes or until they're cooked through. Remove the meatballs and set them aside.

3. Stir the orzo in the saucepot and cook for 5 minutes. Stir the escarole in the saucepot. Return the meatballs to the saucepot and cook until they're heated through. Sprinkle with the cheese.

MAKES 10 SERVINGS

Kitchen Tip: The secret to this recipe's flavor is the cheese, add a tablespoon or two to the finished soup to enhance the flavor!

Vegetable-Chicken Noodle Soup

  1   cup chopped celery
 ½   cup thinly sliced leek (white part only)
 ½   cup chopped carrot
 ½   cup chopped turnip
  6   cups chicken broth, divided
  1   tablespoon minced fresh parsley
1½   teaspoons fresh thyme *or* ½ teaspoon dried thyme
  1   teaspoon minced fresh rosemary leaves *or* ¼ teaspoon dried rosemary
  1   teaspoon balsamic vinegar
 ¼   teaspoon black pepper
  2   ounces uncooked yolk-free wide noodles
  1   cup boneless skinless chicken breast, cooked and diced

1. Combine celery, leek, carrot, turnip and ⅓ cup broth in large saucepan. Cover; cook over medium heat 12 to 15 minutes or until vegetables are tender, stirring occasionally.

2. Stir in remaining 5⅔ cups broth, parsley, thyme, rosemary, vinegar and pepper; bring to a boil. Add noodles; cook until noodles are tender.

3. Stir in chicken. Reduce heat to medium; simmer until heated through.

MAKES 6 SERVINGS

Fruit Salad with Creamy Banana Dressing

2   cups fresh pineapple chunks
1   cup cantaloupe cubes
1   cup honeydew melon cubes
1   cup fresh blackberries
1   cup sliced fresh strawberries
1   cup seedless red grapes
1   medium apple, diced
2   medium ripe bananas, sliced
½   cup vanilla nonfat Greek yogurt
2   tablespoons honey
1   tablespoon lemon juice
¼   teaspoon ground nutmeg

1. Combine pineapple, cantaloupe, honeydew, blackberries, strawberries, grapes and apple in large bowl; gently toss.

2. Combine bananas, yogurt, honey, lemon juice and nutmeg in blender or food processor; blend until smooth.

3. Pour dressing over fruit mixture; gently toss to coat. Serve immediately.

MAKES 8 SERVINGS

Warm Chutney Chicken Salad

Nonstick olive oil cooking spray
6   ounces boneless skinless chicken breasts, cut into bite-size pieces
⅓   cup mango chutney
¼   cup water
1   tablespoon Dijon mustard
4   cups packaged mixed salad greens
1   cup chopped peeled mango or papaya
Sliced green onions (optional)

1. Spray medium skillet with cooking spray; heat over medium-high heat. Add chicken; cook and stir 2 to 3 minutes or until cooked through. Stir in chutney, water and mustard; cook and stir until heated through. Cool slightly.

2. Toss together salad greens and mango. Arrange on serving plates. Spoon chicken mixture onto greens. Garnish with green onions.

MAKES 2 SERVINGS

Fruit Salad with Creamy Banana Dressing

Pumpkin Soup with Crumbled Bacon and Toasted Pumpkin Seeds

2 teaspoons olive oil

½ cup raw pumpkin seeds

1 onion, chopped

1 teaspoon kosher salt

½ teaspoon chipotle chili powder

½ teaspoon black pepper

2 cans (29 ounces each) solid-pack pumpkin

4 cups chicken broth

¾ cup apple cider

½ cup whipping cream

Sour cream (optional)

3 slices thick-sliced bacon, crisp-cooked and crumbled

Slow Cooker Directions

1. Heat oil in medium skillet over medium heat. Add pumpkin seeds and stir until seeds begin to pop, about 1 minute. Transfer to small bowl; set aside.

2. Add onion to same skillet; cook and stir over medium heat until translucent. Stir in salt, chipotle chili powder and black pepper. Transfer to slow cooker. Whisk in pumpkin, broth and apple cider; stir until smooth. Cover; cook on HIGH 4 hours.

3. Turn off heat. Whisk in whipping cream and adjust seasonings. Strain and keep warm until serving. Garnish with sour cream, toasted pumpkin seeds and crumbled bacon.

MAKES 4 TO 6 SERVINGS

tip

Pumpkin seeds (or "pepitas") are a common ingredient in Mexican cooking. They can be purchased raw or roasted and salted; either variety may be found hulled or whole.

Pumpkin Soup with Crumbled Bacon
and Toasted Pumpkin Seeds

Italian Bread Salad

3   slices (½-inch-thick) day-old whole wheat bread
½   cup buttermilk
1   small clove garlic, minced
1   tablespoon minced fresh dill *or* 1 teaspoon dried dill weed
1½ teaspoons onion powder
¼   teaspoon black pepper
2   large tomatoes, cored and cut into 1-inch cubes
1   small cucumber, peeled, cut lengthwise into halves, seeded and thinly sliced
1   small stalk celery, thinly sliced
2   tablespoons minced fresh parsley
⅛   teaspoon salt

1. Preheat oven to 400°F. Cut bread into 1-inch pieces; place on baking sheet. Bake 5 to 7 minutes or until lightly toasted and dry, stirring occasionally. Remove from pan; let cool.

2. For dressing, combine buttermilk, garlic, dill, onion powder and pepper in small jar with tight-fitting lid; shake well. Let stand 15 minutes to allow flavors to blend.

3. Combine tomatoes, cucumber, celery and parsley in large bowl; toss. Sprinkle with salt; toss well. Toss toasted bread with vegetables just before serving. Shake dressing; pour over salad and toss to coat.

MAKES 4 SERVINGS

Orange-Onion Salad

1   tablespoon rice vinegar
1   tablespoon soy sauce
2   teaspoons dark sesame oil
1   large navel orange, peeled and sliced
1   small red onion, thinly sliced
    Romaine lettuce or spinach leaves
    Carrot curls (optional)

1. Combine vinegar, soy sauce and sesame oil in small bowl; stir to blend.

2. Place orange and onion slices in single layer in shallow baking dish; drizzle with soy sauce mixture. Cover; refrigerate at least 30 minutes or up to 8 hours.

3. Transfer orange and onion slices to lettuce-lined serving platter or individual lettuce-lined dishes; drizzle with juices from dish. Garnish with carrot curls.

MAKES 4 SERVINGS

Italian Bread Salad

Greens, White Bean and Barley Soup

2 tablespoons olive oil

3 carrots, diced

1½ cups chopped onions

2 cloves garlic, minced

1½ cups sliced mushrooms

6 cups vegetable broth

2 cups cooked barley

1 can (about 15 ounces) Great Northern beans, rinsed and drained

2 whole bay leaves

1 teaspoon sugar

1 teaspoon dried thyme

7 cups chopped stemmed collard greens (about 24 ounces)

1 tablespoon white wine vinegar

Hot pepper sauce

Red bell pepper strips (optional)

1. Heat oil in Dutch oven over medium heat. Add carrots, onions and garlic; cook and stir 3 minutes. Add mushrooms; cook and stir 5 minutes or until carrots are tender.

2. Add broth, barley, beans, bay leaves, sugar and thyme; bring to a boil over high heat. Reduce heat to medium-low; cover and simmer 5 minutes. Add greens; simmer 10 minutes. Remove and discard bay leaves. Stir in vinegar. Season with hot pepper sauce. Garnish with red bell peppers.

MAKES 8 SERVINGS

Greens, White Bean and Barley Soup

Chicken Caesar Salad

  4   small boneless skinless chicken breasts

  6   ounces uncooked gnocchi or other dried pasta

  1   package (9 ounces) frozen artichoke hearts, thawed

1½ cups cherry tomatoes, quartered

 ¼ cup plus 2 tablespoons plain yogurt

  2   tablespoons mayonnaise

  2   tablespoons grated Romano cheese

  1   tablespoon dry sherry or red wine vinegar

  1   clove garlic, minced

 ½ teaspoon anchovy paste

 ½ teaspoon Dijon mustard

 ½ teaspoon white pepper

  1   small head romaine lettuce, torn into bite-size pieces

  1   cup toasted bread cubes

1. Prepare grill for direct cooking over medium-high heat. Grill chicken 5 to 7 minutes or until no longer pink in center; set aside.

2. Cook pasta according to package directions, omitting salt. Drain and rinse well under cold water until pasta is cool; drain well. Combine pasta, artichoke hearts and tomatoes in large bowl; set aside.

3. Combine yogurt, mayonnaise, Romano cheese, sherry, garlic, anchovy paste, mustard and pepper in small bowl; whisk until smooth. Add to pasta mixture; toss to coat evenly.

4. Arrange lettuce on platter or individual plates. Spoon pasta mixture over lettuce. Thinly slice chicken breasts and place on top of pasta. Sprinkle with bread cubes.

MAKES 4 SERVINGS

Chicken Caesar Salad

Chicken Tortilla Soup

4   (6-inch) corn tortillas, cut into strips
1   tablespoon corn oil
1   pound chicken tenders, cut into bite-size pieces
2   cups chicken broth
1   tablespoon SPICE ISLANDS® Minced Onion
2   teaspoons SPICE ISLANDS® Garlic Powder
2   teaspoons SPICE ISLANDS® Chili Powder
1   teaspoon SPICE ISLANDS® Fine Grind Black Pepper
1   can (15 ounces) black beans, rinsed and drained
1   can (14½ ounces) diced tomatoes with green chilies
½   cup julienned carrots
2   cups (8 ounces) shredded Cheddar cheese

BAKE tortilla strips on a baking sheet in a preheated 350°F oven for 7 to 10 minutes, until crisp.

HEAT oil in large heavy saucepan. Stir-fry chicken 3 to 5 minutes, or until no longer pink in center. Add broth, onion, garlic powder, chili powder and pepper. Bring to a boil over medium heat. Reduce heat and simmer 5 minutes. Stir in black beans, tomatoes, carrots and tortilla strips (reserve a few tortilla strips for garnish).

SIMMER for 20 minutes. Add Cheddar cheese.

LADLE into soup bowls. Sprinkle remaining tortilla strips on top of soup bowls; dollop with sour cream, if desired.

MAKES 6 SERVINGS

Pear and Cranberry Salad

½   cup canned whole berry cranberry sauce

2   tablespoons balsamic vinegar

1   tablespoon olive or canola oil

12   cups (9 ounces) packed assorted bitter or gourmet salad greens

6   small or 4 large ripe pears (about 1¾ pounds), cored and cut into ½-inch-thick slices

½   cup blue or Gorgonzola cheese, crumbled

1. Combine cranberry sauce, vinegar and oil in small bowl; mix well.

2. Arrange greens on six serving plates. Arrange pears over greens; drizzle with dressing. Sprinkle with cheese. Serve immediately.

MAKES 6 SERVINGS

Cook's Notes: Be sure to use ripe pears. Forelles and Red Bartletts are particularly well suited for use in this salad.

Carrot Raisin Salad with Citrus Dressing

¾   cup sour cream

¼   cup milk

1   tablespoon honey

1   tablespoon lime juice

1   tablespoon thawed frozen orange juice concentrate

    Grated peel of 1 medium orange

¼   teaspoon salt

8   medium carrots, peeled and coarsely shredded (about 2 cups)

¼   cup raisins

⅓   cup chopped cashew nuts

1. Stir sour cream, milk, honey, lime juice, orange juice concentrate, orange peel and salt in medium bowl until smooth and well blended.

2. Combine carrots and raisins in large bowl. Add dressing; toss to coat. Cover and refrigerate 30 minutes. Gently toss before serving. Top with cashews.

MAKES 8 SERVINGS

Carrot Raisin Salad
with Citrus Dressing

Minestrone Soup

¾ cup uncooked small shell pasta

2 cans (about 14 ounces each) vegetable broth

1 can (28 ounces) crushed tomatoes in tomato purée

1 can (about 15 ounces) white beans, rinsed and drained

1 package (16 ounces) frozen vegetable medley, such as broccoli, green beans, carrots and red peppers

4 to 6 teaspoons prepared pesto

1. Cook pasta according to package directions. Drain.

2. Meanwhile, combine broth, tomatoes and beans in Dutch oven. Cover and bring to a boil over high heat. Reduce heat to low; simmer 3 to 5 minutes.

3. Add vegetables to broth mixture and return to a boil over high heat. Stir in pasta; simmer until vegetables and pasta are heated through. Ladle soup into bowls; spoon about 1 teaspoon pesto in center of each serving.

MAKES 4 TO 6 SERVINGS

Classic French Onion Soup

¼ cup (½ stick) butter

3 large yellow onions, sliced

1 cup dry white wine

3 cans (about 14 ounces each) beef or chicken broth

1 teaspoon Worcestershire sauce

½ teaspoon salt

½ teaspoon dried thyme

4 slices French bread, toasted

1 cup (4 ounces) shredded Swiss cheese

Sprigs fresh thyme (optional)

Slow Cooker Directions

1. Melt butter in large skillet over medium heat. Add onions, cook and stir 15 minutes or until onions are soft and lightly browned. Stir in wine.

2. Combine onion mixture, broth, Worcestershire sauce, salt and dried thyme in slow cooker. Cover; cook on LOW 4 to 4½ hours.

3. Ladle soup into four bowls; top each with bread slice and ¼ cup cheese. Garnish with thyme sprig.

MAKES 4 SERVINGS

Minestrone Soup

Green Salad with Pears and Pecans

¼ cup mayonnaise

¼ cup sour cream

¾ tablespoon balsamic vinegar

1 tablespoon olive oil

1 tablespoon finely minced onion

⅛ teaspoon black pepper

Salt

1 bag (10 ounces) mixed salad greens

2 ripe pears, cored and thinly sliced

1 cup (4 ounces) finely shredded Swiss cheese

½ cup pecans, toasted*

Pomegranate seeds (optional)

To toast pecans, spread in single layer in heavy skillet. Cook and stir over medium heat 1 to 2 minutes or until nuts are lightly browned.

1. Combine mayonnaise, sour cream, vinegar, oil, onion and pepper in small bowl. Season with salt; stir to blend. Set aside.

2. Arrange greens evenly on four plates. Place pear slices around edges of plates. Sprinkle cheese and pecans over greens. Drizzle dressing evenly over salads. Garnish with pomegranate seeds.

MAKES 4 SERVINGS

Green Salad with Pears and Pecans

Sherried Oyster and Brie Soup

- 1 cup cream sherry
- 1 quart select Maryland oysters with liquor
- 2 tablespoons butter
- 1 pound mushrooms, thinly sliced
- ½ cup minced shallots
- 2 tablespoons lemon juice
- 2 tablespoons all-purpose flour
- 3 cups beef broth
- 4 ounces Brie cheese
- 1 cup milk
- 1 cup whipping cream
- Salt and white pepper
- Chopped fresh chives (optional)

1. Bring sherry to a boil in small saucepan over medium-high heat. Reduce heat to low. Simmer until slightly thickened and reduced to ½ cup. Set aside.

2. Drain oysters, reserving liquor. Set aside.

3. Melt butter in large saucepan over medium-high heat. When foam subsides, stir in mushrooms, shallots and lemon juice; cook and stir 2 minutes. Sprinkle with flour; cook and stir 1 minute. Add broth and reduced sherry; bring to a boil. Reduce heat to low; simmer 20 minutes.

4. Cut Brie cheese into wedges; using paring knife, remove and discard outer white rind. Stir in cheese until melted. Stir in reserved oyster liquor, milk, cream, salt and pepper; cook until heated through. *Do not boil.* Remove from heat; add oysters. Cover; let stand until oysters are just plumped. Garnish with chives.

MAKES 4 SERVINGS

Sherried Oyster and Brie Soup

Heartwarming
BREADS

Bacon Cheddar Monkey Bread

1¾ cups (7 ounces) shredded sharp Cheddar cheese

12 ounces bacon, cooked and chopped (about 1 cup)

¼ cup finely chopped green onions

2¾ to 3 cups all-purpose flour, divided

1 package (¼ ounce) rapid-rise active dry yeast

1 teaspoon salt

1 cup warm water (120°F)

2 tablespoons olive oil

⅓ cup butter, melted

1 egg

1. Combine cheese, bacon and green onions in medium bowl; mix well.

2. Combine 1½ cups flour, yeast and salt in large bowl of electric stand mixer; stir to combine. Add water and oil; beat at medium speed 3 minutes with paddle attachment.

3. Replace paddle attachment with dough hook; beat in 1¼ cups flour until dough comes together. Add 1 cup cheese mixture; knead at medium-low speed 6 to 8 minutes or until dough is smooth and elastic, adding remaining ¼ cup flour if necessary to clean side of bowl. Place dough in greased bowl; turn dough so top is greased. Cover and let rise in warm place 30 minutes or until doubled in size.

4. Generously spray 12-cup (10-inch) bundt pan with nonstick cooking spray. Whisk butter and egg in shallow bowl until blended. Punch down dough. Roll 1-inch pieces of dough into balls. Dip balls in butter mixture; roll in remaining cheese mixture to coat. Layer balls in prepared pan. Cover; let rise in warm place 40 minutes or until almost doubled in size. Preheat oven to 375°F.

5. Bake 35 minutes or until golden brown. Loosen edges of bread with knife; invert onto wire rack. Cool 5 minutes; serve warm.

MAKES 12 SERVINGS

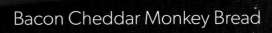
Bacon Cheddar Monkey Bread

Pumpkin-Ginger Scones

½ cup sugar, divided

2 cups all-purpose flour

2 teaspoons baking powder

1 teaspoon ground cinnamon

½ teaspoon baking soda

½ teaspoon salt

¼ cup (½ stick) cold butter, cut into small pieces

1 egg

½ cup solid-pack pumpkin

¼ cup sour cream

½ teaspoon grated fresh ginger *or* 2 tablespoons finely chopped crystallized ginger

1 tablespoon butter, melted

1. Preheat oven to 425°F.

2. Reserve 1 tablespoon sugar. Combine remaining sugar, flour, baking powder, cinnamon, baking soda and salt in large bowl. Cut in ¼ cup butter with pastry blender or two knives until mixture resembles coarse crumbs. Beat egg in small bowl. Add pumpkin, sour cream and ginger; beat until well blended. Stir pumpkin mixture into flour mixture until it forms soft dough that leaves side of bowl.

3. Turn dough out onto well-floured surface. Knead ten times. Roll dough using floured rolling pin into 9×6-inch rectangle. Cut into six 3-inch squares. Cut each square diagonally in half, making 12 triangles; place 2 inches apart on ungreased baking sheets. Brush tops of triangles with melted butter and sprinkle with reserved sugar.

4. Bake 10 to 12 minutes or until golden brown. Cool 10 minutes on wire racks. Serve warm.

MAKES 12 SCONES

Pumpkin-Ginger Scones

Banana Bran Bread

1 cup bran cereal

½ cup boiling water

1⅓ cups all-purpose flour

1 teaspoon baking powder

½ teaspoon baking soda

¼ teaspoon salt

¼ teaspoon ground cinnamon

2 tablespoons vegetable oil

⅓ cup plus 2 tablespoons sugar

2 eggs, beaten

1 cup ripe mashed bananas (2 medium to large bananas)

¼ cup crumbled unsweetened banana chips

½ cup chopped walnuts or pecans

1. Preheat oven to 350°F. Coat 8½-inch loaf pan with nonstick cooking spray.

2. Pour cereal into heatproof bowl. Stir in boiling water. Let stand 10 minutes. Combine flour, baking powder, baking soda, salt and cinnamon in large bowl. Combine oil, sugar and eggs in separate large bowl; beat well. Stir in flour mixture and bran; mix well. Stir in mashed bananas.

3. Spoon batter into prepared pan. Sprinkle with banana chips and walnuts. Bake 45 to 50 minutes or until toothpick inserted into center comes out clean. Cool bread in pan 5 minutes. Turn out onto wire rack. Cool completely.

MAKES 1 LOAF

Variation: Fold in ½ cup dried fruit, such as raisins or cranberries.

Banana Bran Bread

Baked Doughnuts with Cinnamon Glaze

    5   to 5½ cups all-purpose flour, divided
    ⅔   cup granulated sugar
    2   packages (¼ ounce each) active dry yeast
    1   teaspoon salt
    1   teaspoon grated lemon peel
    ½   teaspoon ground nutmeg
    2   cups milk, divided
    ½   cup (1 stick) butter
    2   eggs
    2   cups sifted powdered sugar
    ½   teaspoon ground cinnamon

1. Combine 2 cups flour, granulated sugar, yeast, salt, lemon peel and nutmeg in large bowl. Combine 1¾ cups milk and butter in 1-quart saucepan. Heat over low heat until mixture is 120° to 130°F. (Butter does not need to completely melt.) Gradually beat milk mixture into flour mixture with electric mixer at low speed. Increase speed to medium; beat 2 minutes.

2. Beat in eggs and 1 cup flour at low speed. Increase speed to medium; beat 2 minutes. Stir in enough additional flour, about 2 cups, to make soft dough. Cover with greased plastic wrap; refrigerate at least 2 hours or up to 24 hours.

3. Punch down dough. Turn out dough onto lightly floured surface. Knead dough 1 minute or until dough is no longer sticky, adding remaining ½ cup flour to prevent sticking, if necessary.

4. Grease two large baking sheets. Roll out dough to ½-inch thickness with lightly floured rolling pin. Cut dough with floured 2½-inch doughnut cutter. Reroll scraps, reserving doughnut holes. Place doughnuts and holes 2 inches apart on prepared baking sheets. Cover with towels; let rise in warm place 30 minutes or until doubled in bulk.

5. To prepare glaze, combine powdered sugar and cinnamon in small bowl. Stir in enough remaining milk, about ¼ cup, to make glaze of desired consistency. Cover; set aside.

6. Preheat oven to 400°F. Place pieces of waxed paper under wire racks. Bake doughnuts and holes 8 to 10 minutes or until golden brown. Remove from pan; cool on wire racks 5 minutes. Dip warm doughnuts into glaze. Place right side up on racks, allowing glaze to drip down sides. Serve warm.

MAKES 2 DOZEN DOUGHNUTS AND HOLES

Baked Doughnuts with Cinnamon Glaze

Pull-Apart Rye Rolls

¾ cup water

2 tablespoons butter, softened

2 tablespoons molasses

2¼ cups all-purpose flour, divided

½ cup rye flour

⅓ cup nonfat dry milk powder

1 package (¼ ounce) active dry yeast

1½ teaspoons salt

1½ teaspoons caraway seeds

Melted butter

1. Heat water, 2 tablespoons softened butter and molasses in small saucepan over low heat until temperature reaches 120°F. Combine 1¼ cups all-purpose flour, rye flour, milk powder, yeast, salt and caraway seeds in large bowl. Stir heated water mixture into flour mixture with wooden spoon to form soft, sticky dough. Gradually add additional all-purpose flour until rough dough forms.

2. Turn out dough onto lightly floured surface. Knead 5 to 8 minutes or until smooth and elastic, gradually adding remaining flour to prevent sticking, if necessary. Cover with inverted bowl. Let rise 35 to 40 minutes or until dough has increased in bulk by one third.

3. Punch down dough; divide in half. Roll each half into 12-inch log. Using sharp knife, cut each log evenly into 12 pieces; shape into tight balls. Arrange in greased 8- or 9-inch round baking pan. Brush tops with melted butter. Loosely cover with lightly greased sheet of plastic wrap. Let rise in warm place 45 minutes or until doubled in bulk.

4. Preheat oven to 375°F. Uncover rolls; bake 15 to 20 minutes or until golden brown. Cool in pan on wire rack 5 minutes. Remove to wire rack; cool completely.

MAKES 24 ROLLS

Pull-Apart Rye Rolls

Glazed Espresso Chocolate Marble Bread

   4   cups all-purpose flour
   2   teaspoons baking powder
   1   teaspoon baking soda
   ½   teaspoon salt
1½   cups (3 sticks) butter, softened
   2   cups sugar
   4   eggs
   1   tablespoon vanilla
   2   cups sour cream
   1   tablespoon plus ½ teaspoon instant espresso powder *or* instant coffee powder, divided
   5   tablespoons hot water, divided
   ¼   cup unsweetened cocoa powder
   ½   cup semisweet chocolate chips
   ¼   cup whipping cream

1. Preheat oven to 350°F. Grease three 8×4-inch loaf pans with butter or spray with nonstick cooking spray.

2. Combine flour, baking powder, baking soda and salt in small bowl. Beat butter in large bowl with electric mixer until light and creamy. Add sugar; beat 2 minutes. Beat in eggs and vanilla. Beat in half of flour mixture until well blended. Add sour cream; beat 1 minute or until well blended. Beat in remaining half of flour mixture.

3. Remove half of batter to medium bowl. Stir 1 tablespoon espresso powder into 2 tablespoons hot water in small bowl until smooth; add to one bowl of batter and mix well. Blend cocoa and remaining 3 tablespoons water in small bowl until smooth; stir into remaining bowl of batter until well blended. Drop large spoonfuls of batter from each bowl alternately into prepared loaf pans. Swirl through batter once or twice with skewer or tip of knife.

4. Bake 45 to 50 minutes or until toothpick inserted into centers comes out clean. Cool in pans on wire racks 10 minutes. Remove from pans; cool completely on wire racks.

5. Combine chocolate chips, cream and remaining ½ teaspoon espresso powder in medium microwavable bowl. Microwave on HIGH 20 seconds; stir until smooth. (If necessary, microwave at additional 15-second increments until chocolate melts.) Drizzle glaze over tops of loaves. Bread may be made up to two days in advance.

MAKES 3 LOAVES

Tip: Disposable foil pans are a great solution if you do not have three loaf pans. 9×5-inch pans can be used instead of 8×4-inch pans; loaves will be slightly shorter.

Glazed Espresso Chocolate Marble Bread

Raspberry Breakfast Ring

½   cup warm milk (105° to 115°F)

⅓   cup warm water (105° to 115°F)

1   package (¼ ounce) active dry yeast

3   to 3¼ cups all-purpose flour, divided

1   egg

3   tablespoons butter, melted

3   tablespoons granulated sugar

1   teaspoon salt

¼   cup red raspberry fruit spread

1   teaspoon grated orange peel

⅓   cup powdered sugar

2   teaspoons orange juice

1. Combine milk, water and yeast in large bowl of electric stand mixer. Let stand 5 minutes. Add 2¾ cups flour, egg, butter, granulated sugar and salt; beat at medium-low speed with dough hook until soft dough forms. Knead 6 minutes or until dough is smooth and elastic, adding remaining flour, if necessary, to prevent sticking. Place dough in greased bowl; turn to grease top. Cover; let rise in warm place 45 to 60 minutes or until doubled in size.

2. Punch dough down. Cover; let rest in warm place 10 minutes. Line large baking sheet with parchment paper. Combine fruit spread and orange peel in small bowl; mix well.

3. Roll out dough into 16×9-inch rectangle on lightly floured surface. Spread fruit spread mixture evenly over dough. Starting with long side, roll up dough jelly-roll style; pinch seam to seal. Shape dough into ring on prepared baking sheet, keeping seam side down and pinching ends to seal.

4. Cut slices three fourths of the way through dough at every inch, using serrated knife. Slightly twist each section of the dough out, forming many rings. Cover loosely with plastic wrap and let rise in warm place 30 to 45 minutes or until doubled in size. Preheat oven to 350°F.

5. Bake 25 minutes or until lightly browned. Remove to wire rack to cool completely.

6. Whisk powdered sugar and orange juice in small bowl until well blended. Drizzle over ring. Cut into 16 slices to serve.

MAKES 16 SERVINGS

Potato Rosemary Rolls

2 to 2½ cups all-purpose flour, divided
1½ tablespoons sugar
1 envelope FLEISCHMANN'S® RapidRise Yeast
1¼ teaspoons salt
1 teaspoon dried rosemary, crushed
¾ cup milk
½ cup water
½ cup instant potato flakes or buds
2 tablespoons olive oil
1 egg, lightly beaten
   Sesame or poppy seeds or additional dried rosemary, crushed

In a large bowl, combine ⅔ cup flour, sugar, undissolved yeast, salt and rosemary. Heat milk, water, potato flakes and oil until very warm (120° to 130°F). Gradually add to flour mixture. Beat 2 minutes at medium speed of electric mixer, scraping bowl occasionally. Stir in enough remaining flour to make a soft dough. Knead on lightly floured surface until smooth and elastic, about 8 to 10 minutes. Cover; let rest 10 minutes.

Divide dough into 12 equal pieces. Roll each piece to 10-inch rope; coil each rope and tuck end under coil. Place rolls 2 inches apart on greased baking sheet. Cover; let rise in warm, draft-free place until doubled in size, about 1 hour.

Brush tops with beaten egg; sprinkle with sesame seeds. Bake at 375°F for 15 to 20 minutes or until done. Remove from pan; cool on wire rack.

MAKES 12 ROLLS

Bread Machine Directions: Dough can be prepared in 1½- and 2-pound bread machines. Measure all dough ingredients into bread machine pan in the order suggested by manufacturer, adding potato flakes with flour. Select dough/manual cycle. When cycle is complete, remove dough to floured surface. If necessary, knead in additional flour to make dough easy to handle.

Apricot-Cranberry Holiday Bread

⅔ cup milk

6 tablespoons butter, softened

2½ to 3 cups all-purpose flour, divided

¼ cup sugar

1 package (¼ ounce) active dry yeast

¾ teaspoon salt

½ teaspoon ground ginger

½ teaspoon ground nutmeg

2 eggs, divided

½ cup dried apricots, chopped

½ cup dried cranberries, chopped

3 tablespoons orange juice

½ cup pecans, toasted* and coarsely chopped

1 teaspoon water

To toast pecans, spread in single layer on baking sheet. Bake in preheated 350°F oven 5 to 7 minutes or until lightly browned, stirring occasionally.

1. Heat milk and butter in small saucepan over low heat until temperature reaches 120° to 130°F. Combine 1½ cups flour, sugar, yeast, salt, ginger and nutmeg in large bowl. Slowly add heated milk mixture to flour mixture. Add 1 egg; stir with rubber spatula 2 minutes or until blended. Gradually stir in more flour until dough begins to lose its stickiness, 2 to 3 minutes. Mix apricots, cranberries and orange juice in small microwavable bowl; cover with plastic wrap. Microwave on HIGH 25 to 35 seconds to soften; set aside.

2. Turn out dough onto floured surface. Knead 5 to 8 minutes or until smooth and elastic; gradually add remaining flour to prevent sticking, if necessary. Drain or blot apricot mixture. Combine apricot mixture and pecans in medium bowl. Flatten dough into ¾-inch-thick rectangle; sprinkle with one third of fruit mixture. Roll up jelly-roll style from short end. Flatten dough; repeat twice using remaining fruit mixture. Continue to knead until blended. Shape dough into ball; place in large greased bowl. Turn dough over. Cover; let rise 1 hour or until doubled in size.

3. Grease 9-inch round cake or pie pan. Punch down dough; pat into 8-inch circle. Place in pan. Loosely cover with lightly greased sheet of plastic wrap. Let rise 1 hour or until doubled in size.

4. Preheat oven to 375°F. Beat remaining egg with 1 teaspoon water in small bowl; brush evenly over dough. Bake 30 to 35 minutes or until loaf sounds hollow when tapped. Remove immediately from pan. Cool completely on wire rack.

MAKES 12 SERVINGS

Apricot-Cranberry Holiday Bread

Cinnamon Raisin Bread

4 cups all-purpose flour

2½ teaspoons salt

2½ teaspoons active dry yeast

¼ cup (½ stick) butter

1 cup plus 2 tablespoons milk

2 tablespoons honey

2 eggs

1 cup raisins

2 tablespoons melted butter, divided

8 teaspoons sugar

4 teaspoons ground cinnamon

1. Combine flour, salt and yeast in bowl of electric stand mixer. Melt ¼ cup butter in small saucepan over low heat; stir in milk and honey until mixture is warm but not hot. Whisk in eggs; remove from heat.

2. Add egg mixture and raisins to flour mixture. With dough hook, mix on low speed until dough separates from sides of bowl and forms a ball. Continue mixing 2 minutes.

3. Place dough in lightly oiled bowl, turning to coat top. Cover loosely with plastic wrap. Let rise in warm place 1 to 1½ hours or until dough is doubled in bulk.

4. Grease and flour two 8×4-inch loaf pans. Punch down dough and separate into two balls. Shape each ball into 8×10-inch rectangle. Brush tops of dough with 1 tablespoon melted butter.

5. Combine sugar and cinnamon in small bowl. Reserve 2 teaspoons cinnamon-sugar mixture; sprinkle remaining cinnamon-sugar mixture evenly over dough.

6. Roll up one dough rectangle, starting with short side; place in prepared loaf pan. Repeat with remaining dough. Cover with plastic wrap. Let rise in warm place 1 to 1½ hours or until almost doubled in bulk.

7. Preheat oven to 375°F. Bake loaves 35 minutes or until golden brown, rotating pans once. Brush tops with remaining 1 tablespoon melted butter; sprinkle with reserved cinnamon-sugar mixture. Cool in pans 10 minutes. Remove to wire rack; cool completely.

MAKES 2 LOAVES

Cinnamon Raisin Bread

Dinner Rolls

1¼ cups milk

½ cup shortening

3¾ to 4¼ cups all-purpose flour, divided

¼ cup sugar

2 packages (¼ ounce each) active dry yeast

1 teaspoon salt

2 eggs

1. Combine milk and shortening in small saucepan. Heat over low heat until temperature reaches 120° to 130°F. (Shortening does not need to melt completely.)

2. Combine 1½ cups flour, sugar, yeast and salt in large bowl. Gradually beat milk mixture into flour mixture with electric mixer at low speed until well combined. Beat in eggs and 1 cup flour; beat at medium speed 2 minutes. Using wooden spoon, stir in enough additional flour to make soft dough, about 1¼ cups.

3. Turn out dough onto lightly floured surface. Knead in enough remaining flour 10 minutes or until dough is smooth and elastic.

4. Place dough in large, lightly greased bowl; turn once to coat evenly. Cover with towel; let rise in warm place 1 hour or until doubled in size.

5. Punch down dough. Knead on lightly floured surface 1 minute. Cover with towel; let rest 10 minutes. Grease two 8-inch square baking pans. Cut dough in half. Cut one half into 12 pieces, keeping remaining half covered with towel. Shape pieces into balls; place in rows in one prepared pan. Repeat with remaining dough. Cover pans with towels; let rise in warm place (85°F) 30 minutes or until doubled.

6. Preheat oven to 375°F. Bake 15 to 20 minutes or until golden brown. Remove to wire racks to cool slightly. Serve warm.

MAKES 24 ROLLS

Dinner Rolls

Peanut Butter Chocolate Chip Loaves

     3   cups all-purpose flour
  1½   teaspoons baking powder
     1   teaspoon baking soda
     1   teaspoon salt
     1   cup creamy peanut butter
     ½   cup granulated sugar
     ½   cup packed light brown sugar
     ½   cup (1 stick) butter, softened
     2   eggs
  1½   cups buttermilk*
     2   teaspoons vanilla
     1   cup mini semisweet chocolate chips

Soured fresh milk can be substituted for buttermilk. To sour milk, combine 4½ teaspoons lemon juice plus enough milk to equal 1½ cups. Stir; let stand 5 minutes before using.

1. Preheat oven to 350°F. Spray two 8½×4½-inch loaf pans with nonstick cooking spray.

2. Sift flour, baking powder, baking soda and salt into large bowl. Beat peanut butter, granulated sugar, brown sugar and butter in another large bowl with electric mixer at medium speed until light and fluffy. Beat in eggs, one at a time. Beat in buttermilk and vanilla. Gradually add flour mixture. Beat at low speed until blended. Stir in chocolate chips. Divide batter evenly between prepared pans.

3. Bake 45 minutes or until toothpick inserted into centers comes out clean. Cool in pans on wire racks 10 minutes. Remove from pans and cool completely on wire racks.

MAKES 2 LOAVES

Variation: Stir in ¾ cup chocolate chips before baking; sprinkle with remaining ¼ cup chocolate chips after baking.

Peanut Butter Chocolate Chip Loaves

Prosciutto Provolone Rolls

  3   cups all-purpose flour, divided

  1   package (¼ ounce) rapid-rise active dry yeast

1½ teaspoons salt

  1   cup warm water (120°F)

  2   tablespoons olive oil

 ⅓ cup garlic and herb spreadable cheese

  6   thin slices prosciutto (3-ounce package)

  6   slices (1 ounce each) provolone cheese

1. Combine 1½ cups flour, yeast and salt in large bowl of electric stand mixer; stir to combine. Add water and oil; beat at medium speed 2 minutes with paddle attachment.

2. Replace paddle attachment with dough hook. Add remaining 1½ cups flour; beat at medium speed about 2 minutes to form soft dough that cleans side of bowl. Knead at medium-low speed 6 to 8 minutes or until dough is smooth and elastic. Place dough in greased bowl; turn to grease top. Cover and let rise in warm place 30 minutes or until doubled in size.

3. Punch down dough. Spray 12 standard (2½-inch) muffin cups with nonstick cooking spray. Roll out dough into 12×10-inch rectangle on lightly floured surface.

4. Spread garlic and herb cheese evenly over dough. Arrange prosciutto slices over herb cheese; top with provolone slices. Starting with long side, roll up dough jelly-roll style; pinch seam to seal. Cut crosswise into 1-inch slices; arrange slices, cut sides up, in prepared muffin cups. Cover; let rise in warm place 25 minutes or until nearly doubled in size. Preheat oven to 375°F.

5. Bake 20 minutes or until golden brown. Loosen edges of rolls with knife; remove to wire rack. Serve warm.

MAKES 12 ROLLS

Prosciutto Provolone Rolls

Orange Cinnamon Rolls

- ½ cup packed brown sugar
- 3 tablespoons butter, melted and divided
- 1 tablespoon ground cinnamon
- 1 teaspoon grated orange peel
- 1 loaf (1 pound) frozen bread dough, thawed
- ⅓ cup raisins (optional)
- ½ cup powdered sugar, sifted
- 1 to 2 tablespoons orange juice

1. Grease two 8-inch round cake pans. Combine brown sugar, 1 tablespoon butter, cinnamon and orange peel in small bowl; mix well.

2. Roll out dough on lightly floured surface to 18×8-inch rectangle. Brush dough with remaining 2 tablespoons butter; spread evenly with brown sugar mixture. Sprinkle with raisins, if desired. Starting with long side, roll up dough jelly-roll style; pinch seam to seal. Cut crosswise into 1-inch slices; arrange slices cut sides down in prepared pans. Cover loosely with plastic wrap. Let rise in warm place 30 to 40 minutes or until almost doubled in bulk.

3. Preheat oven to 350°F. Bake 18 minutes or until golden brown. Immediately remove to wire racks; cool slightly.

4. Whisk powdered sugar and orange juice in small bowl until smooth and pourable consistency. Drizzle glaze over warm rolls.

MAKES 18 ROLLS

Cranberry Cheesecake Muffins

- 1 package (3 ounces) cream cheese, softened
- 4 tablespoons sugar, divided
- 1 cup milk
- ⅓ cup vegetable oil
- 1 egg
- 1 package (about 15 ounces) cranberry quick bread mix

1. Preheat oven to 400°F. Grease 12 standard (2½-inch) muffin cups.

2. Beat cream cheese and 2 tablespoons sugar in small bowl until well blended; set aside. Beat milk, oil and egg in large bowl until blended. Stir in quick bread mix just until moistened.

3. Fill prepared muffin cups one fourth full with batter. Drop 1 teaspoon cream cheese mixture into center of each cup. Spoon remaining batter over cream cheese mixture.

4. Sprinkle batter with remaining 2 tablespoons sugar. Bake 17 to 22 minutes or until golden brown. Cool 5 minutes. Remove from muffin cups to wire rack to cool.

MAKES 12 MUFFINS

Orange Cinnamon Rolls

SATISFYING
SIDE DISHES

Harvest Casserole

1   pound bulk pork sausage
2   acorn squash (about 2 pounds each)
1   cup cooked rice
½   cup dried cranberries
½   teaspoon salt
½   teaspoon ground cinnamon
½   teaspoon black pepper
1   can (10¾ ounces) condensed chicken broth, divided

1. Preheat oven to 350°F. Spray 11×7-inch baking dish with nonstick cooking spray.

2. Heat large skillet over medium-high heat. Crumble sausage into skillet; cook and stir 5 minutes or until browned. Drain fat. Place sausage in large bowl.

3. Pierce both squash in several places using sharp knife. Microwave on HIGH 8 minutes, turning over halfway through cooking time. When cool enough to handle, cut ½ inch off top and bottom of each squash. Cut each squash horizontally. Remove seeds and membrane. Place squash halves in prepared baking dish.

4. Combine rice, cranberries, salt, cinnamon and pepper with sausage. Stir in ¼ cup broth. Spoon sausage mixture into squash halves. Pour remaining broth into baking dish around squash.

5. Bake, covered, 15 minutes. Bake, uncovered, 5 to 10 minutes or until squash is tender.

MAKES 4 SERVINGS

Harvest Casserole

Traditional Stuffing

   2 cups sliced celery
   1 cup chopped onion
1½ tablespoons poultry seasoning
   1 teaspoon sage
   ½ teaspoon salt
   ¼ teaspoon black pepper
   2 tablespoons olive oil
   8 cups fresh bread cubes (white, whole-wheat or multi-grain)
   2 cups QUAKER® Oats (quick or old fashioned, uncooked)
   1 cup chopped apple
   1 cup dried cranberries
   ½ cup chopped walnuts
   ¼ cup chopped parsley
   1 can (10¾ ounces) chicken broth

1. Cook celery, onion, poultry seasoning, sage, salt and pepper in oil over medium-low heat 4 to 5 minutes or until tender. Remove from heat.

2. Combine bread cubes, oats, apple, cranberries, walnuts and parsley; mix well.

3. Add onion mixture and chicken broth. Mix until bread is evenly coated.

4. Stuff into body and neck of turkey. Immediately after stuffing, place turkey in oven and begin roasting (according to package directions from turkey).

MAKES 9 CUPS

tip
This is enough stuffing for a 13- to 19-pound turkey. If using a larger turkey, double the recipe and bake any remaining stuffing in a casserole dish for about 1 hour or until warmed through.

Traditional Stuffing

Spinach and Potatoes au Gratin

4   large red potatoes, cut into ¼-inch-thick slices

2   bags (6 ounces each) baby spinach*

2   tablespoons butter, melted

¼   teaspoon salt

⅛   teaspoon black pepper

½   cup whipping cream

⅛   teaspoon ground nutmeg

½   cup grated Parmesan cheese

You may substitute regular spinach, but remove tough stems after washing.

1. Preheat oven to 350°F. Spray 11×7-inch baking dish with nonstick cooking spray. Arrange half of potato slices in prepared dish.

2. Bring large saucepan of water to a boil. Add spinach; cook 30 seconds or until wilted. Drain; rinse under cold water. Squeeze out excess moisture. Place half of spinach on potato slices. Drizzle with melted butter. Sprinkle with half of salt and pepper. Top with remaining potatoes and spinach. Sprinkle with remaining salt and pepper. Combine cream and nutmeg in small bowl; pour over spinach.

3. Bake 40 to 50 minutes or until potatoes are almost tender. Remove from oven; sprinkle with cheese. Bake 15 minutes or until cheese is lightly browned and potatoes are tender. If cheese browns too quickly, cover loosely with foil.

MAKES 6 SERVINGS

Tip: To prepare ahead, bake 50 minutes or until potatoes are tender. Cover; refrigerate up to one day. To serve, sprinkle with cheese and bake 15 to 20 minutes in preheated 350°F oven or until heated through and cheese is lightly browned.

Sautéed Snow Peas & Baby Carrots

1   tablespoon I CAN'T BELIEVE IT'S NOT BUTTER!® Spread

2   tablespoons chopped shallots or onion

5   ounces frozen whole baby carrots, partially thawed

4   ounces snow peas (about 1 cup)

2   teaspoons chopped fresh parsley (optional)

In 12-inch nonstick skillet, melt I Can't Believe It's Not Butter!® Spread over medium heat and cook shallots, stirring occasionally, 1 minute or until almost tender. Add carrots and snow peas and cook, stirring occasionally, 4 minutes or until crisp-tender. Stir in parsley, if desired, and heat through.

MAKES 2 SERVINGS

Spinach and Potatoes au Gratin

Crunchy Asparagus

1 package (10 ounces) frozen asparagus cuts
2 tablespoons water
1 teaspoon lemon juice
3 to 4 drops hot pepper sauce
¼ teaspoon salt
¼ teaspoon dried basil
⅛ teaspoon black pepper
2 teaspoons sunflower kernels
Lemon slices (optional)

Microwave Directions

1. Place asparagus and water in 1-quart microwavable casserole dish; cover. Microwave on HIGH 4½ to 5½ minutes or until asparagus is heated through, stirring halfway through cooking time. Drain. Cover; set aside.

2. Combine lemon juice, hot pepper sauce, salt, basil and black pepper in small bowl; stir to blend. Pour mixture over asparagus; toss to coat. Sprinkle with sunflower kernels. Garnish with lemon slices.

MAKES 4 SERVINGS

Wild Rice Apple Side Dish

1 cup uncooked wild rice
3½ cups chicken broth
½ teaspoon ground nutmeg
1 cup dried apple slices
1 cup chopped onion
1 jar (4.5 ounces) sliced mushrooms, drained
½ cup thinly sliced celery

In large saucepan, simmer wild rice, broth and nutmeg 20 minutes. Add remaining ingredients; cover and simmer 20 to 30 minutes, stirring occasionally, until wild rice reaches desired doneness.

MAKES 6 SERVINGS

Favorite Recipe from **Minnesota Cultivated Wild Rice Council**

Crunchy Asparagus

Kentucky Cornbread & Sausage Stuffing

½   pound BOB EVANS® Original Recipe Roll Sausage

3   cups fresh bread cubes, dried or toasted

3   cups crumbled prepared cornbread

1   large apple, peeled and chopped

1   small onion, chopped

1   cup chicken or turkey broth

2   tablespoons minced fresh parsley

1   teaspoon salt

1   teaspoon rubbed sage or poultry seasoning

¼   teaspoon black pepper

Crumble sausage into small skillet. Cook over medium heat until browned, stirring occasionally. Place sausage and drippings in large bowl. Add remaining ingredients; toss lightly. Use to stuff turkey loosely just before roasting. Or, place stuffing in greased 13×9-inch baking dish. Add additional broth for moister stuffing, if desired. Bake in 350°F oven 30 minutes. Leftover stuffing should be removed from bird and stored separately in refrigerator. Reheat thoroughly before serving.

MAKES ENOUGH STUFFING FOR
5-POUND TURKEY OR 8 SIDE-DISH SERVINGS

Serving Suggestion: Double this recipe to stuff a 12- to 15-pound turkey.

Festive Cranberry Mold

½   cup water

1   package (6 ounces) raspberry-flavored gelatin

1   can (8 ounces) jellied cranberry sauce

1⅔   cups cranberry juice cocktail

1   cup sliced bananas

½   cup walnuts, toasted*

To toast walnuts, spread in single layer on baking sheet. Bake in preheated 350°F oven 5 to 7 minutes or until lightly toasted, stirring occasionally.

1. Bring water to a boil in medium saucepan over medium-high heat. Add gelatin and stir until dissolved. Fold in cranberry sauce. Reduce heat to medium; cook until sauce is melted. Stir in cranberry juice cocktail.

2. Refrigerate mixture until slightly thickened. Fold in banana slices and walnuts. Pour mixture into 4-cup mold; cover and refrigerate until gelatin is set.

MAKES 8 SERVINGS

Kentucky Cornbread & Sausage Stuffing

Orange-Spice Glazed Carrots

1 package (32 ounces) baby carrots
½ cup packed light brown sugar
½ cup orange juice
3 tablespoons butter
¾ teaspoon ground cinnamon
¼ teaspoon ground nutmeg
¼ cup cold water
2 tablespoons cornstarch

Slow Cooker Directions

1. Combine all ingredients except water and cornstarch in slow cooker. Cover; cook on LOW 3½ to 4 hours or until carrots are crisp-tender.

2. Spoon carrots into serving bowl. Turn slow cooker to HIGH.

3. Stir water into cornstarch in small bowl until smooth and well blended. Whisk into slow cooker. Cook, uncovered, on HIGH 10 to 15 minutes or until thickened. Spoon over carrots.

MAKES 6 SERVINGS

Green Bean Casserole

1 can (10¾ ounces) CAMPBELL'S® Condensed Cream of Mushroom Soup (Regular *or* 98% Fat Free)
½ cup milk
1 teaspoon soy sauce
  Dash ground black pepper
2 packages (10 ounces *each*) frozen cut green beans, cooked and drained
1 can (2.8 ounces) French fried onions (1⅓ cups)

1. Stir the soup, milk, soy sauce, black pepper, green beans and ⅔ **cup** onions in a 1½-quart casserole.

2. Bake at 350°F. for 25 minutes or until hot. Stir the green bean mixture.

3. Sprinkle the remaining onions over the green bean mixture. Bake for 5 minutes more or until onions are golden brown.

MAKES 5 SERVINGS

Kitchen Tip: You can also make this classic side dish with fresh or canned green beans. You will need either 1½ **pounds** fresh green beans, cut into 1-inch pieces, cooked and drained, **or 2 cans** (about 16 ounces **each**) cut green beans, drained, for the frozen green beans.

Orange-Spice Glazed Carrots

Roasted Potatoes and Pearl Onions

3   pounds red potatoes, cut into 1½-inch cubes
1   package (10 ounces) pearl onions, peeled
2   tablespoons olive oil
2   teaspoons dried basil or thyme
1   teaspoon paprika
¾   teaspoon salt
¾   teaspoon dried rosemary
¾   teaspoon black pepper

1. Preheat oven to 400°F. Spray large shallow roasting pan* with nonstick cooking spray.

2. Combine potatoes and onions in prepared pan. Drizzle with oil; toss to coat. Combine basil, paprika, salt, rosemary and pepper in small bowl; mix well. Sprinkle over potatoes and onions; toss to coat.

3. Roast 20 minutes. Stir vegetables; roast 15 to 20 minutes or until potatoes are browned and tender when pierced with fork.

Do not use glass baking dish or potatoes will not brown.

MAKES 8 SERVINGS

Golden Apples and Yams

2   large yams or sweet potatoes
2   Washington Golden Delicious apples, cored and sliced crosswise into rings
¼   cup firmly packed brown sugar
1   teaspoon cornstarch
⅛   teaspoon ground cloves
½   cup orange juice
2   tablespoons chopped pecans or walnuts

Heat oven to 400°F. Bake yams 50 minutes or until soft, but still hold their shape. (This can also be done in microwave.) Let yams cool enough to handle. *Reduce oven temperature to 350°F.*

Peel and slice yams crosswise. In shallow 1-quart baking dish, alternate apple rings and yam slices, overlapping edges slightly. In small saucepan, combine sugar, cornstarch and cloves; stir in orange juice until well blended. Heat orange juice mixture over medium heat, stirring until thickened; pour over apples and yams. Sprinkle with nuts; bake 20 minutes or until apples and yams are tender.

MAKES 6 SERVINGS

Favorite Recipe from **Washington Apple Commission**

Roasted Potatoes and Pearl Onions

Old-Fashioned Herb Stuffing

6 slices (8 ounces) whole wheat, rye or white bread (or combination),
     cut into ½-inch cubes
1 tablespoon butter
1 cup chopped onion
½ cup thinly sliced celery
½ cup thinly sliced carrot
1 cup chicken broth
1 tablespoon chopped fresh thyme *or* 1 teaspoon dried thyme
1 tablespoon chopped fresh sage *or* 1 teaspoon dried sage
½ teaspoon paprika
¼ teaspoon black pepper

1. Preheat oven to 350°F. Place bread cubes on baking sheet; bake 10 minutes or until dry.

2. Spray 1½-quart baking dish with nonstick cooking spray.

3. Melt butter in large saucepan over medium heat. Add onion, celery and carrot; cook and stir 10 minutes or until vegetables are tender. Add broth, thyme, sage, paprika and pepper to saucepan; bring to a simmer. Stir in bread cubes. Spoon into prepared dish.

4. Cover; bake 25 to 30 minutes or until heated through.

MAKES 4 SERVINGS

Old-Fashioned Herb Stuffing

Roasted Butternut Squash

Nonstick cooking spray
1 pound butternut squash, peeled and cut into 1-inch cubes (about 4 cups)
2 medium onions, coarsely chopped
8 ounces carrots, peeled and cut into ½-inch diagonal slices (about 2 cups)
1 tablespoon dark brown sugar
¼ teaspoon salt
Black pepper (optional)
1 tablespoon butter, melted

1. Preheat oven to 400°F. Line large baking sheet with foil and spray with cooking spray.

2. Arrange vegetables in single layer on prepared baking sheet; spray with cooking spray. Sprinkle with brown sugar, salt and pepper, if desired.

3. Bake 30 minutes. Gently stir; bake 10 to 15 minutes or until tender. Drizzle with butter; toss to coat.

MAKES 5 SERVINGS

Honey Mustard-Orange Roasted Vegetables

6 cups assorted cut-up vegetables (red or green bell peppers, zucchini, red onions and carrots)
2 tablespoons olive oil
1 teaspoon minced garlic
1 teaspoon salt
¼ cup FRENCH'S® Honey Mustard
2 tablespoons orange juice
1 teaspoon grated orange peel

1. Preheat oven to 450°F. Toss vegetables with oil, garlic and salt in roasting pan.

2. Bake, uncovered, 20 minutes or until tender.

3. Toss vegetables with mustard, juice and orange peel just before serving. Serve over pasta or with bread, if desired.

MAKES 6 SERVINGS

Roasted Butternut Squash

Oyster Stuffing

1½ pounds French bread, cut into 1-inch cubes
¾ cup (1½ sticks) butter
1 clove garlic, minced
1½ cups diced celery
1½ cups diced onions
3 fresh bay leaves, chopped
2 tablespoons fresh thyme
1 tablespoon Old Bay seasoning
10 fresh sage leaves, chopped
1 teaspoon salt
1 teaspoon black pepper
4 cups chicken broth
3 large eggs, beaten
⅓ cup chopped fresh Italian parsley
1½ pints shucked oysters

1. Preheat oven to 350°F. Butter 3-quart covered casserole dish. Place bread cubes in single layer on large baking sheet. Bake 8 to 10 minutes or until bread is golden brown, stirring once during baking. Cool on wire rack.

2. Melt ¾ cup butter in large skillet over medium heat. Add garlic; cook and stir 1 minute. Add celery, onions and bay leaves; cook and stir 6 to 8 minutes or until vegetables are soft. Add thyme, Old Bay seasoning, sage, salt and pepper; cook and stir 1 minute.

3. Combine broth and eggs in medium bowl. Place toasted bread in large bowl; stir in parsley and cooked vegetable mixture. Add oysters and three fourths of broth mixture; stir in gently. Stuffing should be moist but not wet; add remaining broth mixture as necessary. Spoon stuffing into prepared casserole.

4. Cover; bake 30 minutes. Remove cover; bake 20 to 30 minutes or until top of stuffing is golden brown and crisp; center of stuffing should reach 165°F.

MAKES 12 SERVINGS

Tip: Bread can be toasted one day in advance.

Oyster Stuffing

Potato Pancakes with Apple-Cherry Chutney

Apple-Cherry Chutney (recipe follows)
1 pound baking potatoes (about 2 medium), cut into 1-inch pieces
½ small onion
3 egg whites
2 tablespoons all-purpose flour
½ teaspoon salt
¼ teaspoon black pepper
4 teaspoons vegetable oil, divided
Fresh mint

1. Prepare Apple-Cherry Chutney; set aside.

2. Combine potatoes, onion, egg whites, flour, salt and pepper in food processor or blender; process until almost smooth (mixture will appear grainy).

3. Heat large nonstick skillet 1 minute over medium heat. Add 1 teaspoon oil. Spoon ⅓ cup batter per pancake into skillet. Cook three pancakes at a time, 3 minutes per side or until golden brown. Repeat with remaining batter, adding 1 teaspoon oil with each batch. Serve with Apple-Cherry Chutney. Garnish with mint.

MAKES 6 SERVINGS

Apple-Cherry Chutney

1 cup chunky applesauce
½ cup canned tart cherries, drained
2 tablespoons packed brown sugar
1 teaspoon lemon juice
½ teaspoon ground cinnamon
⅛ teaspoon ground nutmeg

Combine applesauce, cherries, brown sugar, lemon juice, cinnamon and nutmeg in small saucepan; bring to a boil. Reduce heat; simmer 5 minutes. Serve warm.

MAKES 1½ CUPS

Potato Pancakes with Apple-Cherry Chutney

Cashew Green Beans

1 tablespoon peanut or vegetable oil
1 small onion, cut into thin wedges
2 cloves garlic, minced
1 package (10 ounces) frozen julienne-cut green beans, thawed, drained and patted dry
2 tablespoons oyster sauce
1 tablespoon rice vinegar
1 tablespoon honey
¼ cup coarsely chopped cashew nuts or peanuts

Heat oil in wok or large skillet over medium-high heat. Add onion and garlic; stir-fry 3 minutes. Add green beans; stir-fry 2 minutes. Add oyster sauce, vinegar and honey; stir-fry 1 minute or until heated through. Remove from heat; stir in cashews.

MAKES 4 SERVINGS

Marinated Mushrooms, Carrots and Snow Peas

1 cup matchstsick-size cut carrots
1 cup fresh snow peas or sugar snap peas
½ cup water
1 lemon
2 cups small mushrooms
⅔ cup white wine vinegar
2 tablespoons sugar
2 tablespoons chopped fresh parsley
2 tablespoons extra virgin olive oil
1 tablespoon chopped fresh thyme
1 clove garlic, minced

1. Combine carrots and peas in 1-quart microwavable dish; add water. Cover; microwave on HIGH 4 minutes or just until water boils. *Do not drain.*

2. Remove several strips of peel from lemon with vegetable peeler. Chop peel to measure 1 teaspoon. Squeeze juice from lemon to measure 2 tablespoons. Combine peel, juice and remaining ingredients in small bowl. Pour over carrot mixture. Cover; refrigerate at least 3 hours.

3. To serve, remove vegetables from marinade with slotted spoon. Place in serving dish; discard marinade.

MAKES 12 SERVINGS

Cashew Green Beans

Southern Pecan Cornbread Stuffing

5 cups dry cornbread stuffing mix
1 package KNORR® Leek Recipe Mix
½ cup (1 stick) I CAN'T BELIEVE IT'S NOT BUTTER!® Spread
1 cup coarsely chopped pecans
1 package (10 ounces) frozen corn, thawed and drained
1 cup hot water
1 cup orange juice

1. Preheat oven to 350°F. In large bowl, combine stuffing and recipe mix.

2. In 8-inch skillet, melt I Can't Believe It's Not Butter!® Spread over medium heat and cook pecans, stirring occasionally, 5 minutes.

3. Add corn, water, orange juice and pecan mixture to stuffing; toss until moistened. Spoon into 2-quart casserole sprayed with cooking spray.

4. Cover and bake 30 minutes or until heated through.

MAKES 8 SERVINGS

Cheddary Garlic Mashed Potatoes

4 cups hot mashed potatoes
1 can (10¾ ounces) condensed cream of chicken soup
1½ cups shredded Cheddar cheese
⅛ teaspoon garlic powder
1½ cups FRENCH'S® French Fried Onions, divided

1. Preheat oven to 375°F. Heat mashed potatoes, soup, *1 cup* cheese and garlic powder in saucepan over medium heat. Stir until cheese melts.

2. Spoon potato mixture into 2-quart baking dish. Top with ½ *cup* cheese and French Fried Onions.

3. Bake 5 to 10 minutes or until hot and onions are golden.

MAKES 6 TO 8 SERVINGS

Southern Pecan Cornbread Stuffing

Chutney'd Squash Circles

2 acorn squash (1 pound each)
2 tablespoons butter
½ cup prepared chutney
2 tablespoons water

1. Preheat oven to 400°F. Slice tip and stem end from each squash; discard. Cut squash crosswise into ¾-inch rings. Scoop out and discard seeds.

2. Tear off 18-inch square of heavy-duty foil. Center foil in 13×9-inch baking dish. Dot foil with butter; place squash on butter, slightly overlapping rings. Spoon chutney over slices; sprinkle with water. Bring foil on long sides of pan together in center, folding over to make tight seam. Fold ends to form tight seal.

3. Bake 20 minutes or until squash is fork-tender. Transfer to warm serving plate. Pour pan drippings over squash.

MAKES 4 SERVINGS

Country Green Beans with Ham

2 teaspoons olive oil
¼ cup finely chopped onion
1 clove garlic, minced
1 pound fresh green beans
1 cup chopped fresh tomatoes
6 slices (2 ounces) thinly sliced ham
1 tablespoon chopped fresh marjoram
2 teaspoons chopped fresh basil
⅛ teaspoon black pepper
¼ cup herbed croutons

1. Heat oil in medium saucepan over medium heat. Add onion and garlic; cook and stir 4 minutes or until onion is tender.

2. Reduce heat to low. Add green beans, tomatoes, ham, marjoram, basil and pepper; cook 10 minutes or until liquid is evaporated, stirring occasionally.

3. Transfer mixture to serving dish. Top with croutons.

MAKES 4 SERVINGS

Chutney'd Squash Circles

Fresh Vegetable Casserole

    8   small new potatoes
    8   baby carrots
    1   head cauliflower, broken into florets
    4   stalks asparagus, cut into 1-inch pieces
    3   tablespoons butter
    3   tablespoons all-purpose flour
    2   cups milk
        Salt and black pepper
    ¾   cup (3 ounces) shredded Cheddar cheese
        Chopped fresh cilantro or parsley

1. Preheat oven to 350°F. Grease 2-quart casserole. Steam potatoes, carrots, cauliflower and asparagus in steamer basket over boiling water 5 to 7 minutes or until crisp-tender. Arrange vegetables in prepared casserole.

2. Melt butter in medium saucepan over medium heat. Stir in flour until smooth. Slowly whisk in milk; bring to a boil. Cook and stir 2 minutes or until thickened and bubbly. Season with salt and pepper. Stir in cheese until melted. Pour over vegetables; sprinkle with cilantro.

3. Bake 15 minutes or until heated through.

MAKES 4 TO 6 SERVINGS

Fresh Vegetable Casserole

Cranberry-Pumpkin Spoonbread

3 cups milk

1 cup cornmeal

6 tablespoons butter

2 tablespoons packed brown sugar

1¼ teaspoons pumpkin pie spice

1 teaspoon baking powder

¾ teaspoon salt

1 can (15 ounces) solid-pack pumpkin

4 eggs, separated

1 cup dried cranberries, coarsely chopped*

Or substitute 1 cup of any dried fruit, such as cherries, blueberries, apricots or combination.

1. Preheat oven to 350°F. Grease 11×7-inch baking pan. Bring milk to a simmer in medium saucepan over medium-high heat. Slowly whisk in cornmeal, stirring until thickened. Remove from heat and stir in butter.

2. Whisk brown sugar, pumpkin pie spice, baking powder and salt in small bowl. Stir into cornmeal mixture until well blended; cool slightly. Stir in pumpkin, egg yolks and cranberries until well blended.

3. Beat egg whites in large bowl with electric mixer at high speed until stiff peaks form. Fold egg whites into cornmeal mixture in three additions. Spoon into prepared pan.

4. Bake 35 minutes or until puffed and golden. Serve warm.

MAKES 8 SERVINGS

Cranberry-Pumpkin Spoonbread

Green Bean Casserole

 2 packages (10 ounces each) frozen green beans, thawed
 1 can (10¾ ounces) condensed cream of mushroom soup, undiluted
 1 tablespoon chopped fresh parsley
 1 tablespoon chopped roasted red peppers
 1 teaspoon dried sage
 ½ teaspoon salt
 ½ teaspoon black pepper
 ¼ teaspoon ground nutmeg
 ½ cup toasted slivered almonds*

To toast almonds, spread in single layer in heavy skillet. Cook over medium heat 1 to 2 minutes or until nuts are lightly browned, stirring frequently.

Slow Cooker Directions

Combine all ingredients except almonds in slow cooker. Cover; cook on LOW 3 to 4 hours. Sprinkle with almonds.

MAKES 4 TO 6 SERVINGS

Sausage Corn Bread Stuffing

 8 ounces bulk pork sausage (regular or spicy)
 ½ cup (1 stick) butter
 2 medium onions, chopped
 2 cloves garlic, minced
 2 teaspoons dried sage
 1 teaspoon poultry seasoning
 1 package (16 ounces) dry corn bread crumbs
1¼ cups chicken broth

1. Brown sausage in large skillet over medium-high heat until no longer pink, stirring to separate meat. Drain sausage on paper towels; set aside. Wipe skillet with paper towels to remove grease. Melt butter in same skillet over medium heat until foamy. Add onions and garlic; cook and stir 10 minutes or until onions are softened. Stir in dried sage and poultry seasoning; cook 1 minute.

2. Combine corn bread crumbs, sausage and onion mixture in large bowl. Drizzle broth over stuffing; toss stuffing lightly until evenly moistened. Transfer to 3-quart casserole.

3. Preheat oven to 350°F. Bake 45 minutes (55 to 60 minutes if refrigerated) or until heated through. For drier stuffing, uncover during last 15 minutes of baking.

MAKES 12 CUPS

Green Bean Casserole

Sweet Potato Gratin

  3   pounds sweet potatoes (about 5 large)

  ½   cup (1 stick) butter, divided

  ¼   cup plus 2 tablespoons packed light brown sugar, divided

  2   eggs

  ⅔   cup orange juice

  2   teaspoons ground cinnamon, divided

  ½   teaspoon salt

  ¼   teaspoon ground nutmeg

  ⅓   cup all-purpose flour

  ¼   cup old-fashioned oats

  ⅓   cup chopped pecans or walnuts

1. Preheat oven to 350°F.

2. Bake sweet potatoes 1 hour or until tender. Let stand 5 minutes. Cut sweet potatoes lengthwise into halves. Scrape pulp from skins into large bowl.

3. Beat sweet potato pulp, ¼ cup butter and 2 tablespoons brown sugar with electric mixer at medium speed until butter is melted. Add eggs, orange juice, 1½ teaspoons cinnamon, salt and nutmeg; beat until smooth. Pour mixture into 1½-quart casserole or six 6-ounce ovenproof ramekins.

4. Combine flour, oats, remaining ¼ cup brown sugar and ½ teaspoon cinnamon in medium bowl. Cut in remaining ¼ cup butter with pastry blender or two knives until mixture resembles coarse crumbs. Stir in pecans. Sprinkle evenly over sweet potatoes.*

5. Bake 25 to 30 minutes or until heated through. For crispier topping, broil 5 inches from heat source 2 to 3 minutes or until golden brown.

MAKES 6 TO 8 SERVINGS

At this point, recipe may be covered and refrigerated up to one day. Let stand at room temperature 1 hour before baking.

Sweet Potato Gratin

Cherry Butternut Squash Stuffing

2 to 3 strips of bacon, finely diced

3 tablespoons butter or margarine

⅓ cup finely chopped onion

1 cup (about ⅓ pound) chopped butternut squash

⅔ cup dried tart cherries

1 tablespoon fresh rosemary or sage leaves, chopped

3 tablespoons almonds or pecans, toasted and finely ground

3 tablespoons dry bread crumbs

3 tablespoons or more chicken or vegetable broth, if necessary

Salt and black pepper to taste

Cook bacon in a large skillet until crisp. Remove to a large mixing bowl. Add butter, onion and squash to bacon drippings. Cook 3 to 4 minutes or until squash is semi-soft. Add cherries and rosemary; continue cooking until squash is soft.

Add squash mixture to bacon. Stir in nuts and bread crumbs. Mix thoroughly. Add broth, one tablespoon at a time, if dressing is dry. Season with salt and pepper to taste.

MAKES 6 SERVINGS

Serving Suggestions: Use to stuff pork chops or a pork tenderloin. This is also a good stuffing for chicken breasts or Cornish hens.

Favorite Recipe from **Cherry Marketing Institute**

Cherry Butternut Squash Stuffing

Green Beans with Toasted Pecans

3 tablespoons I CAN'T BELIEVE IT'S NOT BUTTER!® Spread, melted

1 teaspoon sugar

¼ teaspoon LAWRY'S® Garlic Powder with Parsley

Pinch ground red pepper

Salt to taste

⅓ cup chopped pecans

1 pound green beans

In small bowl, blend I Can't Believe It's Not Butter!® Spread, sugar, garlic powder, pepper and salt.

In 12-inch nonstick skillet, heat 2 teaspoons garlic mixture over medium-high heat and cook pecans, stirring frequently, 2 minutes or until pecans are golden. Remove pecans and set aside.

In same skillet, heat remaining garlic mixture and stir in green beans. Cook, covered, over medium heat, stirring occasionally, 6 minutes or until green beans are tender. Stir in pecans.

MAKES 4 SERVINGS

Orange-Spiked Zucchini and Carrots

1 pound zucchini, cut into ¼-inch-thick slices

1 package (10 ounces) frozen sliced carrots, thawed

1 cup unsweetened orange juice

1 stalk celery, finely chopped

2 tablespoons chopped onion

Salt and black pepper

1. Combine zucchini, carrots, orange juice, celery and onion in large nonstick saucepan. Season with salt and pepper. Simmer, covered, 10 to 12 minutes or until zucchini is tender.

2. Uncover. Continue to simmer, stirring occasionally, until most of the liquid has evaporated.

MAKES 7 SERVINGS

Green Beans with Toasted Pecans

Wild Rice Mushroom Stuffing

½ cup uncooked wild rice

Day-old French bread (about 4 cups), cut into ½-inch cubes

½ cup (1 stick) butter

1 large onion, chopped

1 clove garlic, minced

3 cups sliced mushrooms

½ teaspoon salt

½ teaspoon rubbed sage

½ teaspoon dried thyme

¼ teaspoon black pepper

1 cup chicken broth

½ cup coarsely chopped pecans

Sprigs fresh thyme (optional)

1. Prepare rice according to package directions; set aside.

2. Preheat broiler. Spread bread cubes in single layer on baking sheet. Broil 5 to 6 inches from heat 4 minutes or until lightly toasted, tossing after 2 minutes; set aside.

3. Melt butter in large skillet over medium heat. Add onion and garlic; cook and stir 3 minutes. Add mushrooms; cook 3 minutes, stirring occasionally. Add salt, sage, dried thyme and pepper. Add cooked rice; cook 2 minutes, stirring occasionally. Stir in broth. Add pecans and toasted bread cubes; toss lightly.

4. Transfer to 1½-quart casserole.* Preheat oven to 325°F. Cover casserole with lid or foil. Bake 40 minutes or until heated through. Garnish with thyme sprigs.

*At this point, stuffing may be covered and refrigerated up to 8 hours before baking. Bake, covered, 50 minutes or until heated through.

MAKES 6 TO 8 SERVINGS

Wild Rice Mushroom Stuffing

MERRY MERRY
MEATS

Glazed Roast Pork Loin
with Cranberry Stuffing

1¼   cups chopped fresh or partially thawed frozen cranberries

2   teaspoons sugar

½   cup (1 stick) butter

1   cup chopped onion

1   package (8 ounces) herb-seasoned stuffing mix

1   cup chicken broth

½   cup diced peeled orange

1   egg, beaten

½   teaspoon grated orange peel

1   (2½- to 3-pound) boneless center cut pork loin roast, butterflied and tied

¼   cup currant jelly

1   tablespoon cranberry liqueur

1. Toss cranberries with sugar in small bowl; set aside. Melt butter in saucepan over medium heat until foamy. Add onion; cook and stir until tender. Remove from heat. Combine stuffing mix, broth, orange, egg and orange peel in large bowl. Add cranberry mixture and onion; toss lightly.

2. Preheat oven to 325°F. Untie roast; spread roast with one fourth of stuffing. Close halves together and re-tie. Place leftover stuffing in covered casserole; bake with roast during last 45 minutes of cooking time. Place roast on meat rack in foil-lined roasting pan. Insert meat thermometer into pork.

3. Combine jelly and liqueur in small bowl. Brush half of mixture over roast after first 45 minutes of roasting. Roast 30 minutes or until internal temperature reaches 165°F when tested with meat thermometer inserted into thickest part of roast. Brush with remaining jelly mixture. Remove roast to cutting board. Cover loosely with foil; let stand 10 to 15 minutes before carving. (Internal temperature will continue to rise 5° to 10°F during stand time.) Carve roast crosswise; serve with stuffing.

MAKES 8 TO 10 SERVINGS

Glazed Roast Pork Loin with Cranberry Stuffing

Beef Rib Roast with Mushroom-Bacon Sauce

- 4 to 5 cloves garlic
- 1 tablespoon kosher salt
- 1 tablespoon chopped fresh thyme
- 1 tablespoon chopped fresh basil
- 1 tablespoon black pepper
- 3 tablespoons olive oil
- 1 beef rib roast (6 to 8 pounds), trimmed
  Mushroom-Bacon Sauce (recipe follows)

1. Place garlic, salt, thyme, basil and pepper in food processor or blender; process until garlic is finely chopped. Add oil in slow stream, processing until paste forms.

2. Pat roast dry; place bone side down on rack in shallow roasting pan. Cut several small slits in fat layer across top of roast. Rub garlic paste over entire roast. Cover; refrigerate at least 4 hours or up to one day.

3. Preheat oven to 450°F. Cook 20 minutes. *Reduce oven temperature to 350°F.* Cook 1 hour 30 minutes or until meat thermometer inserted into center registers 140°F for medium rare or 150°F for medium. Remove roast to large cutting board. Cover loosely with foil; let stand 20 minutes before slicing. Meanwhile, prepare Mushroom-Bacon Sauce using reserved pan drippings.

MAKES 4 TO 6 SERVINGS

Mushroom-Bacon Sauce

- 4 slices bacon, chopped
- 1 shallot, diced
- 1 pound sliced mushrooms
- 6 cups beef broth
- 1 cup dry red wine
- 2 tablespoons butter
  Salt and black pepper

1. Cook bacon in medium saucepan over medium heat until brown. Add shallot; cook and stir 2 minutes. Add mushrooms; cook and stir 8 minutes or until bacon is crisp. Set aside.

2. Bring broth and wine to a boil in large saucepan over medium-high heat. Reduce heat to low; simmer 20 minutes or until mixture is reduced to about 2 cups. (This can be done up to two days ahead. Cover both mushroom mixture and broth mixture separately and refrigerate.)

3. Place reserved roasting pan over two stovetop burners. Add mushroom mixture and broth mixture; cook and stir over medium heat 5 minutes or until sauce is slightly thickened. Whisk in butter; season with salt and pepper.

MAKES ABOUT 3 CUPS

Beef Rib Roast with Mushroom-Bacon Sauce

Browned Pork Chops with Gravy

½ teaspoon dried sage

½ teaspoon dried marjoram

¼ teaspoon black pepper

⅛ teaspoon salt

4 boneless pork loin chops (¾ pound), trimmed of fat

Olive oil cooking spray

¼ cup chopped onion

1 clove garlic, minced

1 cup sliced mushrooms

¾ cup beef broth

⅓ cup sour cream

1 tablespoon all-purpose flour

1 teaspoon Dijon mustard

2 cups hot cooked yolk-free wide egg noodles

Chopped fresh Italian parsley (optional)

1. Combine sage, marjoram, pepper and salt in small bowl. Rub onto both sides of chops. Spray large skillet with cooking spray; heat over medium heat. Add chops; cook 5 minutes or until barely pink in center, turning once. Remove to plate; keep warm.

2. Add onion and garlic to same skillet; cook and stir 2 minutes. Add mushrooms and broth; bring to a boil. Reduce heat to medium-low; cover and simmer 3 to 4 minutes or until mushrooms are tender.

3. Whisk together sour cream, flour and mustard in medium bowl. Whisk in about 3 tablespoons broth mixture from skillet. Stir sour cream mixture into skillet; cook and stir until mixture comes to a boil. Serve gravy over pork chops and noodles. Garnish with parsley.

MAKES 4 SERVINGS

Dad's Dill Beef Roast

1 boneless beef chuck roast (3 to 4 pounds)

1 large jar whole dill pickles, undrained

Hot cooked mashed potatoes

Slow Cooker Directions

Place beef in slow cooker. Pour pickles with juice over top of beef. Cover; cook on LOW 8 to 10 hours. Shred beef with two forks. Serve over potatoes.

MAKES 6 TO 8 SERVINGS

Browned Pork Chops with Gravy

London Broil with Marinated Vegetables

¾   cup olive oil

¾   cup dry red wine

2   tablespoons finely chopped shallots

2   tablespoons red wine vinegar

2   teaspoons bottled minced garlic

½   teaspoon dried thyme

½   teaspoon dried oregano

½   teaspoon dried basil

½   teaspoon black pepper

2   pounds boneless beef top round (London broil) steaks (1½ inches thick)

1   medium red onion, cut into ¼-inch-thick slices

1   package (8 ounces) sliced mushrooms

1   medium red bell pepper, cut into strips

1   medium zucchini, cut into ¼-inch-thick slices

1. Whisk oil, wine, shallots, vinegar, garlic, thyme, oregano, basil and black pepper in medium bowl. Combine London broil and ¾ cup marinade in large resealable food storage bag. Seal bag; turn to coat. Marinate in refrigerator up to 24 hours, turning bag once or twice.

2. Combine onion, mushrooms, bell pepper, zucchini and remaining marinade in separate large resealable food storage bag. Seal bag; turn to coat. Refrigerate up to 24 hours, turning bag once or twice.

3. Preheat broiler. Remove beef from marinade and place on broiler pan; discard marinade. Broil 4 to 5 inches from heat 9 minutes per side or until desired doneness. Let stand 10 minutes before slicing. Cut meat into thin slices.

4. Meanwhile, drain vegetables and arrange on broiler pan; discard marinade. Broil 4 to 5 inches from heat 9 minutes or until edges of vegetables just begin to brown. Serve beef and vegetables immediately on large platter.

MAKES 6 SERVINGS

London Broil with Marinated Vegetables

Cranberry-Onion Pork Roast

1 boneless pork loin roast (about 2 pounds)
1 can (16 ounces) whole cranberry sauce
1 package (1 ounce) dry onion soup mix

Season roast with salt and black pepper; place over indirect heat on grill. Stir together cranberry sauce and onion soup mix and heat, covered, in microwave until hot (about 1 minute). Baste roast with cranberry mixture every 10 minutes until roast is done, about 40 minutes (20 minutes per pound); until internal temperature on a thermometer reads 145°F, followed by a 3-minute rest time.

Remove roast from heat; let rest about 10 minutes before slicing to serve.

Heat any leftover basting mixture to boiling; stir and boil for 5 to 10 minutes and serve alongside roast.

MAKES 4 TO 6 SERVINGS

Favorite Recipe from **National Pork Board**

Peppered Steak with Dijon Sauce

4 boneless beef top loin (New York strip) steaks, cut 1 inch thick (about 1½ pounds)
1 tablespoon FRENCH'S® Worcestershire Sauce
   Crushed black pepper
⅓ cup mayonnaise
⅓ cup FRENCH'S® Honey Dijon Mustard
3 tablespoons dry red wine
2 tablespoons minced red or green onion
2 tablespoons minced fresh parsley
1 clove garlic, minced

1. Brush steaks with Worcestershire and sprinkle with pepper to taste; set aside. To prepare Dijon sauce, combine mayonnaise, mustard, wine, onion, parsley and garlic in medium bowl.

2. Place steaks on grid. Grill steaks over high heat 15 minutes for medium rare or to desired doneness, turning often. Serve with Dijon sauce. Garnish as desired.

MAKES 4 SERVINGS

Tip: Dijon sauce is also great served with grilled salmon and swordfish. To serve with fish, substitute white wine for red wine and minced dill for fresh parsley.

Cranberry-Onion Pork Roast

Rib-Eye Steaks with Sautéed Grape Tomatoes and Brie

2 beef rib-eye steaks, cut 1-inch thick (about 12 ounces each)
2 cups grape tomato halves (about 10 ounces)
3 tablespoons water
3 teaspoons minced prepared roasted garlic, divided
4 ounces Brie cheese, shredded
2 tablespoons thinly sliced fresh basil
   Fresh basil (optional)

1. Combine tomatoes, water and 1 teaspoon garlic in large nonstick skillet. Cook, covered, over medium heat 4 to 5 minutes or until tomatoes are tender, stirring often. Season with salt and pepper, as desired. Remove from skillet; keep warm. Carefully wipe out skillet with paper towels.

2. Press remaining 2 teaspoons garlic evenly onto beef steaks. Place steaks in skillet over medium heat; cook 12 to 15 minutes for medium rare (145°F) to medium (160°F) doneness, turning occasionally.

3. Carve steaks into slices; season with salt and pepper, as desired. Add cheese and basil to tomatoes; stir until well combined. Serve immediately with beef. Garnish with additional basil, if desired.

MAKES 2 TO 4 SERVINGS

Cook's Tips: Two beef top loin (strip) steaks, cut 1-inch thick, may be substituted for rib-eye steaks. Cook 12 to 15 minutes, turning occasionally. To make Brie cheese easier to shred, place in freezer for about 30 minutes.

Favorite Recipe Courtesy **The Beef Checkoff**

Beef Roast and Onion Gravy

2   tablespoons vegetable oil

2   tablespoons chopped onions

3   cloves garlic, minced

⅛   teaspoon dried parsley flakes

½   teaspoon ground black pepper

3½ cups SWANSON® Beef Stock

1   beef eye round roast (about 3 pounds)

⅓   cup all-purpose flour

1. Heat the oil in a 10-inch skillet over medium-high heat. Add the onion, garlic, parsley and black pepper and cook until the onion is tender-crisp, stirring often. Stir the stock in the skillet and heat to a boil. Remove the skillet from the heat.

2. Place the beef in a roasting pan and brush with the stock mixture. Roast at 350°F. for 1 hour or to desired doneness, brushing occasionally with the stock mixture. Remove the beef from the roasting pan.

3. Stir the flour in the skillet. Stir the flour mixture in the roasting pan. Cook and stir over medium heat until the mixture boils and thickens. Serve the gravy with the beef.

MAKES 12 SERVINGS

Stuffed Pork Tenderloin with Apple Relish

6 tablespoons (¾ stick) butter

1 onion, chopped

3 cloves garlic

1 cup dry bread crumbs

1 tablespoon chopped fresh parsley

2 teaspoons minced fresh thyme

1 teaspoon minced fresh sage

½ teaspoon salt, divided

¼ teaspoon black pepper

1 egg, lightly beaten

3 to 4 tablespoons dry white wine or apple cider

2 pork tenderloins (about 1 pound each)

Apple Relish (recipe follows)

1. Preheat oven to 450°F. Place rack in large roasting pan; spray with nonstick cooking spray.

2. Melt butter in large skillet. Add onion and garlic; cook and stir 2 to 3 minutes or until translucent. Add bread crumbs, parsley, thyme, sage, ¼ teaspoon salt and pepper; mix well. Stir in egg. Add enough wine to moisten stuffing.

3. Trim fat from tenderloins. Cut tenderloins in half horizontally about halfway through and open flat. Cover with plastic wrap; pound to ½-inch thickness.

4. Sprinkle tenderloins with remaining ¼ teaspoon salt. Spoon half of stuffing down center of each tenderloin. Close meat around stuffing; tie with kitchen string every 3 or 4 inches to secure. Place in prepared pan.

5. Bake 15 minutes. *Reduce heat to 350°F.* Bake 45 minutes or until cooked through (145°F). Meanwhile, prepare Apple Relish. Serve with pork.

MAKES 8 SERVINGS

Apple Relish

3 large apples, cut into ½-inch pieces

½ cup chopped green onions

½ cup golden raisins

¼ cup chopped crystallized ginger

¼ cup cider vinegar

3 tablespoons sugar

1 tablespoon Irish whiskey

1 tablespoon chopped fresh mint

Combine all ingredients except mint in medium saucepan. Cook, partially covered, over medium heat 20 to 30 minutes or until apples are tender but not falling apart. Let cool. Stir in mint. Serve warm or cold.

MAKES ABOUT 2 CUPS

Peppery Beef Rib Roast

1 beef rib roast (2 to 4 ribs), small end, chine (back) bone removed (6 to 8 pounds)
1 can (14 to 14½ ounces) ready-to-serve beef broth
2 teaspoons chopped fresh thyme
Salt

Rub

2 tablespoons pepper seasoning blend
2 tablespoons minced garlic

1. Heat oven to 350°F. Combine Rub ingredients in small bowl; reserve 2 tablespoons for au jus. Press remaining Rub evenly onto all surfaces of beef roast.

2. Place roast, fat side up, in shallow roasting pan. Insert ovenproof meat thermometer so tip is centered in thickest part of beef, not resting in fat or touching bone. Do not add water or cover. Roast in 350°F oven 2¼ to 2½ hours for medium rare; 2¾ to 3 hours for medium doneness.

3. Remove roast when meat thermometer registers 135°F for medium rare; 150°F for medium. Transfer roast to carving board; tent loosely with aluminum foil. Let stand 15 to 20 minutes. (Temperature will continue to rise about 10°F to reach 145°F for medium rare; 160°F for medium.)

4. Combine broth and reserved rub in small saucepan; bring to a boil. Reduce heat; simmer 5 minutes. Stir in thyme; continue simmering 2 minutes.

5. Carve roast into slices. Season with salt, as desired. Serve with au jus.

MAKES 8 TO 10 SERVINGS

Favorite Recipe Courtesy **The Beef Checkoff**

Pork Chop & Wild Rice Bake

1 package (6 ounces) seasoned long grain & wild rice mix
1⅓ cups FRENCH'S® French Fried Onions, divided
1 package (10 ounces) frozen cut green beans, thawed and drained
¼ cup orange juice
1 teaspoon grated orange peel
4 boneless pork chops (1 inch thick)

1. Preheat oven to 375°F. Combine rice mix and seasoning packet, *2 cups water,* ⅔ cup French Fried Onions, green beans, orange juice and orange peel in 2-quart shallow baking dish. Arrange pork chops on top.

2. Bake, uncovered, 30 minutes or until pork chops are no longer pink in center. Sprinkle chops with remaining ⅔ *cup* onions. Bake 5 minutes or until onions are golden.

MAKES 4 SERVINGS

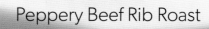
Peppery Beef Rib Roast

Lamb Chops with Cranberry-Pear Chutney

½ cup water

¼ cup dried cranberries

¼ cup dried apricots, cut into quarters

¼ cup raspberry fruit spread

1 tablespoon red wine vinegar

¼ teaspoon ground cinnamon

¼ teaspoon plus ⅛ teaspoon salt, divided

1 medium pear, peeled and cut into ½-inch pieces

½ teaspoon vanilla

4 bone-in lamb loin chops (about 5 ounces each)

2 cloves garlic, minced

¼ teaspoon dried rosemary, crushed

Black pepper

1. Preheat broiler. For chutney, combine water, cranberries, apricots, fruit spread, vinegar, cinnamon and ⅛ teaspoon salt in medium saucepan; bring to a boil over high heat. Reduce heat to medium-low. Simmer, uncovered, 12 minutes or until mixture is thickened. Remove from heat; stir in pear and vanilla.

2. Rub both sides of lamb chops with garlic. Sprinkle with remaining ¼ teaspoon salt and rosemary. Season with pepper. Spray broiler pan and rack with nonstick cooking spray; arrange lamb chops on prepared rack.

3. Broil lamb at least 5 inches from heat source 7 minutes. Turn and broil 7 minutes or until desired doneness. Serve lamb chops with chutney.

MAKES 4 SERVINGS

Beefed-Up Swedish Meatballs

1 pound Ground Beef

¼ cup seasoned dry bread crumbs

1 packet (1 to 1.4 ounces) dry onion soup mix, divided

2 egg whites or 1 whole egg

¼ teaspoon ground nutmeg

¼ teaspoon pepper

2 cups milk

1 tablespoon cornstarch

2 tablespoons water

Hot cooked pasta

Freshly chopped parsley (optional)

1. Combine Ground Beef, bread crumbs, 2 tablespoons onion soup mix, egg whites, nutmeg and pepper in large bowl, mixing lightly but thoroughly. Shape into 12 (1½-inch) meatballs. Heat large nonstick skillet over medium heat until hot. Place meatballs in skillet; cook 17 to 19 minutes, turning occasionally to brown evenly on all sides. Remove from pan; keep warm.

2. Pour off excess drippings from skillet, if necessary. Add milk and remaining onion soup mix to same skillet, stirring until browned bits attached to bottom of skillet are dissolved. Combine cornstarch and water; add to skillet. Bring to a boil. Cook and stir 1 to 2 minutes or until sauce is thickened, stirring frequently. Return meatballs to skillet; cook 3 to 4 minutes or until heated through.

3. Serve over pasta. Sprinkle with parsley, if desired.

MAKES 4 SERVINGS

Favorite Recipe Courtesy **The Beef Checkoff**

Tenderloin Deluxe with Mushroom Sauce

10 tablespoons I CAN'T BELIEVE IT'S NOT BUTTER!® Spread, divided

¼ cup chopped green onions

1 tablespoon Dijon-style mustard

1 teaspoon soy sauce

1 (2½- to 3-pound) beef tenderloin

8 ounces mushrooms, sliced

2 medium onions, finely chopped

2 cloves garlic, finely chopped

⅓ cup dry sherry

4 drops hot pepper sauce

1 cup beef broth

Preheat oven to 425°F.

In small bowl, blend 4 tablespoons I Can't Believe It's Not Butter!® Spread, green onions, mustard and soy sauce. In 13×9-inch baking or roasting pan, arrange beef and evenly spread with mustard mixture.

Bake, uncovered, 15 minutes. Decrease heat to 400°F and bake 45 minutes or until desired doneness. Let stand 10 minutes before slicing.

Meanwhile, in 12-inch skillet, melt remaining 6 tablespoons I Can't Believe It's Not Butter!® Spread over medium-high heat and cook mushrooms, stirring occasionally, 3 minutes or until softened. Stir in onions and cook, stirring occasionally, 12 minutes or until golden brown. Add garlic and cook 30 seconds. Stir in sherry and hot pepper sauce and cook 2 minutes. Stir in broth and simmer 5 minutes or until sauce is slightly thickened. Serve sauce over sliced beef.

MAKES 6 SERVINGS

Tenderloin Deluxe with Mushroom Sauce

Pork Roast with
Dried Cranberries and Apricots

1   center-cut pork loin roast (about 3½ pounds)

1½   cups cranberry-apple juice, divided

1   cup chardonnay or other dry white wine

1½   teaspoons ground ginger

1   teaspoon ground cardamom

2   tablespoons apricot preserves

¼   cup water

1   tablespoon plus 1 teaspoon cornstarch

½   cup dried cranberries

½   cup chopped dried apricots

2   tablespoons golden raisins

1. Place pork roast in large resealable food storage bag. Combine 1 cup cranberry-apple juice, chardonnay, ginger and cardamom in medium bowl. Pour over roast, turning to coat. Seal bag. Marinate in refrigerator 4 hours or overnight, turning several times.

2. Preheat oven to 350°F. Remove roast from marinade; reserve marinade. Place roast in roasting pan. Pour marinade over roast. Bake, loosely covered with foil, 1 hour. Remove foil; continue baking 30 minutes or until internal temperature of roast reaches 165°F when tested with meat thermometer inserted into thickest part of roast, not touching bone. Remove roast to cutting board. Cover loosely with foil. (Internal temperature will continue to rise 5° to 10°F during stand time.)

3. Measure juices from pan. Add enough remaining cranberry-apple juice to equal 1½ cups. Combine juices and apricot preserves in small saucepan. Stir water into cornstarch in small bowl until smooth; stir into juice mixture. Bring to a boil over medium heat. Cook until thickened, stirring frequently. Add dried cranberries, apricots and raisins; cook 2 minutes. Remove from heat.

4. Cut roast into thin slices. Pour sauce over roast slices; serve with any remaining sauce.

MAKES 10 SERVINGS

Pork Roast with Dried Cranberries and Apricots

Pot Roast Carbonnade

6 thick slices applewood-smoked or other smoked bacon (about 6 ounces)

2 tablespoons all-purpose flour

¾ teaspoon salt

½ teaspoon black pepper

1 beef chuck arm pot roast* (about 3½ pounds)

3 large Spanish onions (about 2 pounds), thinly sliced

2 tablespoons packed light brown sugar

1 can (about 14 ounces) beef broth

1 bottle (12 ounces) beer (not dark)

2 teaspoons dried thyme

2 bay leaves

Boiled red potatoes and steamed baby carrots (optional)

*A well-trimmed, 3-pound boneless beef chuck shoulder pot roast can be substituted; however, the bone in the chuck arm roast will give the sauce more flavor.

1. Preheat oven to 350°F. Cook bacon in Dutch oven over medium heat until crisp. Drain bacon on paper towels, reserving drippings in Dutch oven. Crumble bacon; set aside.

2. Combine flour, salt and ½ teaspoon pepper in small bowl; spread on sheet of waxed paper. Place pot roast on flour mixture; roll to coat well. Place pot roast in drippings in Dutch oven. Brown over medium-low heat about 4 to 5 minutes per side. Remove to platter.

3. Pour off all but 2 tablespoons drippings from Dutch oven. Add onions to drippings in Dutch oven; cover and cook 10 minutes over medium heat, stirring once. Uncover; sprinkle with brown sugar. Cook onions, uncovered, over medium-high heat 10 minutes or until golden brown and tender, stirring frequently.

4. Add broth, beer, thyme and bay leaves to Dutch oven; bring to a boil. Return pot roast with any accumulated juices to Dutch oven. Remove from heat; spoon sauce over top. Cover and bake 2 to 2 hours 15 minutes until meat is fork-tender.

5. Remove meat to large cutting board. Cover loosely with foil.

6. Remove and discard bay leaves. Skim fat from juices with large spoon; discard. Place half of juice mixture in food processor or blender; process until smooth. Repeat with remaining juice mixture; return mixture to Dutch oven. Stir reserved bacon into sauce; cook over medium heat until heated through.

7. Discard bone from roast; carve roast into ¼-inch-thick slices with carving knife. Spoon sauce over roast. Serve with potatoes and carrots, if desired.

MAKES 8 SERVINGS

Pot Roast Carbonnade

Beef Tenderloin with Roasted Vegetables

1   boneless beef tenderloin roast (about 3 pounds), trimmed of fat

½   cup chardonnay or other dry white wine

½   cup soy sauce

2   cloves garlic, sliced

1   tablespoon fresh rosemary leaves

1   tablespoon Dijon mustard

1   teaspoon dry mustard

1   pound small red or white potatoes, cut into 1-inch pieces

1   pound brussels sprouts

1   package (12 ounces) baby carrots

1. Place roast in large resealable food storage bag. Combine wine, soy sauce, garlic, rosemary, Dijon mustard and dry mustard in small bowl; stir to blend. Pour over roast. Seal bag; turn to coat. Marinate in refrigerator 4 to 12 hours, turning several times.

2. Preheat oven to 425°F. Spray 13×9-inch baking pan with nonstick cooking spray. Place potatoes, brussels sprouts and carrots in pan. Remove roast from marinade. Pour marinade over vegetables; toss to coat. Cover vegetables with foil; roast 30 minutes. Stir.

3. Place tenderloin on vegetables. Roast, uncovered, 35 to 45 minutes or until internal temperature of roast reaches 135°F for medium-rare to 150°F for medium when tested with meat thermometer inserted into thickest part of tenderloin.

4. Remove tenderloin to large cutting board. Cover loosely with foil; let stand 10 to 15 minutes before carving. (Internal temperature will continue to rise 5° to 10°F during stand time.) Reserve drippings from roasting pan to make gravy, if desired.

5. Stir vegetables; continue roasting if not tender. Slice tenderloin; arrange on large serving platter with roasted vegetables.

MAKES 10 SERVINGS

Orange Beef Steak

1 jar (12 ounces) CAMPBELL'S® Slow Roast Beef Gravy

1 tablespoon grated orange zest

2 tablespoons orange juice

½ teaspoon garlic powder *or* 2 cloves garlic, minced

1 boneless beef top round steak, 1½-inch thick (about 1½ pounds)

1. Stir the gravy, orange zest, orange juice and garlic powder in a 1-quart saucepan.

2. Heat the broiler. Place the beef on a rack in a broiler pan. Broil 4 inches from the heat for 25 minutes for medium or to desired doneness, turning the beef over halfway through cooking and brushing often with the gravy mixture. Thinly slice the beef.

3. Heat the remaining gravy mixture over medium-high heat to a boil. Serve the gravy mixture with the beef.

MAKES 6 SERVINGS

Peppered Beef Rib-Eye Roast

1½ tablespoons black peppercorns

1 boneless beef rib-eye roast (about 2½ to 3 pounds), well trimmed

¼ cup Dijon mustard

2 cloves garlic, minced

Sour Cream Sauce (recipe follows)

1. Prepare grill for indirect cooking over medium heat with drip pan in center.

2. Place peppercorns in small resealable food storage bag. Squeeze out excess air; close bag securely. Pound peppercorns using flat side of meat mallet or rolling pin until cracked.

3. Pat roast dry with paper towels. Combine mustard and garlic in small bowl; spread over roast. Sprinkle with pepper.

4. Place roast on grid directly over drip pan. Grill, covered, 1 hour or until internal temperature reaches 135°F for medium rare or 150°F for medium when tested with meat thermometer inserted into the thickest part of roast. (If using charcoal grill, add four to nine briquets to both sides of the fire after 45 minutes to maintain medium heat.)

5. Meanwhile, prepare Sour Cream Sauce. Cover; refrigerate until serving.

6. Remove roast to large cutting board. Cover loosely with foil; let stand 10 to 15 minutes before carving. (Internal temperature will continue to rise 5° to 10°F during stand time.) Serve with Sour Cream Sauce.

MAKES 6 TO 8 SERVINGS

Sour Cream Sauce

¾ cup sour cream

2 tablespoons prepared horseradish

1 tablespoon balsamic vinegar

½ teaspoon sugar

Combine sour cream, horseradish, vinegar and sugar in small bowl; mix well.

MAKES ABOUT 1 CUP

Peppered Beef Rib-Eye Roast

Veal Escallops with
Fruited California Wild Rice Stuffing

- 3⅓ cups cooked California wild rice
- 1 cup chopped dried apricots
- ½ cup butter, softened, divided
- ½ cup fresh bread crumbs
- ½ cup chopped nuts, toasted (optional)
- 2 egg whites
- 4 tablespoons raisins
  Salt and black pepper to taste
- 10 boned veal cutlets (3 ounces each), pounded thin
- ½ pound shiitake mushrooms, sliced
- ½ cup minced shallots
- 2 teaspoons minced fresh thyme
  All-purpose flour
- 2 cups dry white wine

Mix wild rice, apricots, ¼ cup butter, bread crumbs, nuts, if desired, egg whites, raisins, salt and pepper in medium bowl. Spread approximately ½ cup mixture on each cutlet; roll each cutlet and tie with string. Set aside. Sauté mushrooms and shallots in remaining ¼ cup butter 5 minutes in large saucepan. Season with thyme, salt and pepper. Remove mushroom mixture from pan; set aside. Flour rolled cutlets; brown in same pan. Add wine and mushroom mixture; cover and braise 15 minutes over low heat. Slice and serve with mushroom sauce.

MAKES 10 SERVINGS

Favorite Recipe from **California Wild Rice Advisory Board**

Baked Holiday Ham
with Cranberry-Wine Compote

2 teaspoons peanut oil

⅔ cup chopped onion

½ cup chopped celery

1 cup dry red wine

1 cup honey

½ cup sugar

1 package (12 ounces) fresh cranberries

1 fully cooked smoked ham (10 pounds)

Whole cloves

1. Heat oil in large saucepan over medium-high heat. Add onion and celery; cook and stir until tender. Stir in wine, honey and sugar; bring to a boil. Add cranberries; return to a boil. Reduce heat to low; cover and simmer 10 minutes. Cool completely.

2. Reserve 1 cup clear syrup from cranberry mixture. Transfer remaining cranberry mixture to small serving bowl; cover and refrigerate.

3. Slice away skin from ham with sharp utility knife. (Omit step if meat retailer has already removed skin.)

4. Preheat oven to 325°F. Score fat on ham in diamond design with sharp utility knife; stud with whole cloves. Place ham, fat side up, on rack in shallow roasting pan.

5. Bake, uncovered, 1½ hours. Baste ham with reserved cranberry-wine syrup. Bake 1 to 2 hours more or until meat thermometer inserted into thickest part of ham, not touching bone, registers 140°F, basting with cranberry-wine syrup twice.*

6. Remove ham to large cutting board; let stand 10 minutes. Transfer to large warm serving platter. Slice ham and serve with chilled cranberry-wine compote.

MAKES 16 TO 20 SERVINGS

Total cooking time for ham should be 18 to 24 minutes per pound.

Fajita Pork Tenderloin

1   packet (1.25 ounces) ORTEGA® Reduced Sodium Fajita Seasoning Mix
1   2½- to 3-pound pork tenderloin roast
2   tablespoons olive oil
1   green bell pepper, sliced
1   yellow bell pepper, sliced
1   large onion, sliced
1   pouch (7 ounces) ORTEGA® Fajita Skillet Sauce

PREHEAT oven to 400°F. Rub fajita seasoning mix over rinsed and patted pork tenderloin.

HEAT oil in large skillet over medium-high heat. Add pork and brown 10 minutes, turning until all sides have been browned.

PLACE bell peppers and onion in shallow casserole dish; add seared pork. Pour skillet sauce and ½ cup water over top. Bake 40 minutes or until an instant-read thermometer reads 145°F.

REMOVE from oven; allow to rest 5 minutes before slicing. Serve with bell peppers, onion and sauce.

MAKES 4 TO 6 SERVINGS

Tip: Beans and rice make excellent side dishes for pork roast.

Herb-Roasted Racks of Lamb

½   cup mango chutney, chopped
2   to 3 cloves garlic, minced
2   whole racks (6 ribs each) lamb loin chops (2½ to 3 pounds)
1   cup fresh French or Italian bread crumbs
1   tablespoon chopped fresh thyme *or* 1 teaspoon dried thyme
1   tablespoon chopped fresh rosemary leaves *or* 1 teaspoon dried rosemary
1   tablespoon chopped fresh oregano *or* 1 teaspoon dried oregano

1. Preheat oven to 400°F. Combine chutney and garlic in small bowl; spread evenly over meaty side of lamb. Combine remaining ingredients in separate small bowl; pat crumb mixture evenly over chutney mixture.

2. Place lamb racks, crumb sides up, on rack in shallow roasting pan. Roast 30 to 35 minutes for medium or until internal temperature reaches 145°F when tested with meat thermometer inserted into thickest part of lamb, not touching bone.

3. Remove lamb to large cutting board; tent with foil. Let stand 10 to 15 minutes before carving. (Internal temperature will continue to rise 5° to 10°F during stand time.) Using large knife, slice between ribs into individual chops. Serve immediately.

MAKES 4 SERVINGS

Fajita Pork Tenderloin

Beef Stroganoff

8 ounces uncooked egg noodles

¼ cup all-purpose flour

½ teaspoon salt

¼ teaspoon black pepper

1¼ pounds boneless beef tenderloin steaks or tenderloin tips

4 tablespoons butter, divided

¾ cup chopped onion

12 ounces mushrooms, sliced

1 can (10½ ounces) condensed beef broth

2 tablespoons tomato paste

1 tablespoon Worcestershire sauce

1 cup sour cream, at room temperature

Chopped fresh chives (optional)

1. Cook noodles according to package directions; drain and keep warm.

2. Meanwhile, combine flour, salt and pepper in large resealable food storage bag. Cut steaks into 1½×½-inch strips; add half of beef to flour mixture. Seal bag; shake to coat. Repeat with remaining beef. Discard flour mixture.

3. Melt 1 tablespoon butter in large nonstick skillet over medium-high heat. Add half of beef to skillet; cook and stir until browned on all sides. *Do not overcook.* Transfer to medium bowl. Repeat with 1 tablespoon butter and remaining beef; transfer to same bowl. Set aside.

4. Melt remaining 2 tablespoons butter in same skillet over medium-high heat. Add onion; cook 5 minutes, stirring occasionally. Add mushrooms; cook and stir 5 minutes or until mushrooms are tender.

5. Stir in broth, tomato paste and Worcestershire sauce; bring to a boil, scraping up any browned bits. Return beef and any accumulated juices to skillet; cook about 5 minutes or until heated through and sauce is thickened. Stir in sour cream; heat through. *Do not boil.* Serve beef mixture over noodles. Garnish with chives.

MAKES 4 SERVINGS

Beef Stroganoff

Spice-Rubbed Beef Brisket

2 cups hickory chips

1 teaspoon salt

1 teaspoon paprika

1 teaspoon chili powder

1 teaspoon garlic pepper

1 beef brisket (3 to 3½ pounds)

¼ cup beer or beef broth

1 tablespoon Worcestershire sauce

1 tablespoon balsamic vinegar

1 teaspoon olive oil

¼ teaspoon dry mustard

6 ears corn, cut into 2-inch pieces

12 small new potatoes

6 carrots, cut into 2-inch pieces

2 green bell peppers, cut into 2-inch squares

6 tablespoons lemon juice

6 tablespoons water

1½ teaspoons Italian seasoning

1. Soak hickory chips in water 30 minutes. Prepare grill for indirect cooking over medium heat. Bank briquets on either side of water-filled drip pan.

2. Combine salt, paprika, chili powder and garlic pepper in small bowl; stir to blend. Rub spice mixture onto both sides of brisket. Loosely cover with foil and set aside. Combine beer, Worcestershire sauce, vinegar, oil and dry mustard in small bowl; set aside.

3. Drain hickory chips; sprinkle ½ cup over coals. Place brisket on grid directly over drip pan. Grill, covered, 30 minutes. Baste with reserved beer mixture. Grill 3 hours or until meat thermometer reaches 160°F when inserted into thickest part of brisket, turning every 30 minutes and adding four to nine briquets and ¼ cup hickory chips to each side of fire every hour.

4. Alternately thread corn, potatoes, carrots and bell peppers onto metal skewers. Combine lemon juice, water and Italian seasoning in small bowl; brush onto vegetables. Grill vegetables with brisket 20 to 25 minutes or until tender, turning once.

5. Remove brisket to large cutting board. Cover loosely with foil; let stand 10 minutes before carving. Remove excess fat. Serve beef with vegetable kabobs.

MAKES 12 SERVINGS

Spice-Rubbed Beef Brisket

Dijon Pork Roast with Cranberries

¼ teaspoon ground allspice

¼ teaspoon salt

¼ teaspoon ground black pepper

1 boneless pork loin roast (2 to 2½ pounds), trimmed of excess fat

2 tablespoons FRENCH'S® Honey Dijon Mustard

2 tablespoons honey

2 teaspoons grated orange peel

1⅓ cups FRENCH'S® French Fried Onions, divided

1 cup dried cranberries

Slow Cooker Directions

1. Combine allspice, salt and pepper; sprinkle over roast. Place meat in slow cooker. Blend mustard, honey and orange peel; pour over roast. Sprinkle with ⅔ **cup** French Fried Onions and cranberries.

2. Cover and cook on LOW setting for 4 to 6 hours (or on HIGH for 2 to 3 hours) until meat is fork-tender.

3. Remove pork to serving platter. Skim fat from sauce in slow cooker; transfer sauce to serving bowl. Slice meat and serve with fruit sauce; sprinkle with remaining onions.

MAKES 6 SERVINGS

Note: Cook times vary depending on type of slow cooker used. Check manufacturer's recommendations for cooking pork roast.

Classic Standing Beef Rib Roast

1 (7- to 8-pound) beef standing rib roast

¼ teaspoon ground black pepper

½ cup SWANSON® Beef Stock (Regular or Unsalted)

3 tablespoons red wine

1. Heat the oven to 325°F. Season the beef with the black pepper. Place the beef into a roasting pan, rib-side down.

2. Roast for 2 hours 20 minutes for medium-rare or until desired doneness. Remove the beef to a cutting board and let stand for 20 minutes.

3. Spoon off any fat from the pan drippings. Stir the stock and wine, if desired, in the pan. Cook and stir over medium-high heat until the sauce is reduced slightly, scraping up the browned bits from the bottom of the pan. Season with additional black pepper, if desired. Serve the stock mixture with the beef.

MAKES 8 SERVINGS

Dijon Pork Roast with Cranberries

Veal Chops with
Brandied Apricots and Pecans

¼ cup water

¼ cup honey

8 dried apricot halves, cut into ¼-inch slivers

4 (¾-inch-thick) boneless veal chops (about 5 ounces each)*

¼ teaspoon salt

¼ teaspoon black pepper

3 tablespoons all-purpose flour

2 tablespoons butter

16 pecan halves

2 tablespoons brandy

*If boneless chops are unavailable, bone-in chops can be substituted.

1. Combine water and honey in 2-cup glass measuring cup; microwave on HIGH 2 minutes or until mixture begins to boil. Stir in apricots; cover with plastic wrap, turning back one corner to vent. Microwave 30 seconds; let stand, covered, 1 hour.

2. Sprinkle veal chops with salt and pepper. Place flour in shallow bowl; dredge veal chops, one at a time, shaking off excess.

3. Melt butter in large skillet over medium heat; arrange veal chops and pecan halves in single layer in skillet. Cook veal chops and pecans 5 minutes per side or until browned.

4. Add apricot mixture and brandy; bring to a boil. Reduce heat to low; cover and simmer 10 minutes or until veal chops are cooked through.

5. Transfer veal chops and pecans to serving plates; keep warm. Bring apricot mixture in skillet to a boil over high heat; cook 1 minute or until slightly thickened. To serve, spoon apricot mixture over veal chops.

MAKES 4 SERVINGS

Veal Chops with Brandied Apricots and Pecans

Pork Tenderloin Roast with Fig Sauce

1 tablespoon olive oil
1 pork tenderloin roast (about 1 pound)
1 teaspoon salt
½ teaspoon black pepper
1 jar (about 8 ounces) fig jam or preserves
¼ cup dry red wine

1. Preheat oven to 375°F. Heat oil in large skillet over medium heat; brown pork on all sides. Sprinkle with salt and pepper; place in shallow roasting pan. Roast 15 minutes.

2. Meanwhile, combine fig jam and wine in same skillet; cook and stir over low heat 5 minutes or until melted and warm.

3. Brush small amount of fig sauce over tenderloin; roast 5 to 10 minutes or until temperature reaches 155°F on instant read thermometer. Remove roast to large cutting board. Cover loosely with foil; let stand 10 minutes.

4. Cut pork into thin slices. Serve with remaining fig sauce.

MAKES 4 SERVINGS

Tip: For added flavor, combine 2 cloves minced garlic, 1 teaspoon coarse salt, 1 teaspoon dried rosemary and ¼ teaspoon red pepper flakes. Brush over the pork after browning.

Golden Glazed Flank Steak

1 envelope LIPTON® RECIPE SECRETS® Onion Soup Mix*
1 jar (12 ounces) apricot or peach preserves
½ cup water
1 beef flank steak (about 2 pounds), cut into thin strips
2 medium green, red and/or yellow bell peppers, sliced
  Hot cooked rice

Also terrific with LIPTON® RECIPE SECRETS® Onion Mushroom Soup Mix.

1. In small bowl, combine soup mix, preserves and water; set aside.

2. On foil-lined grid or in broiler pan, without the rack, arrange steak and bell peppers; top with soup mixture.

3. Grill or broil, turning steak and vegetables once, until steak is done. Serve over hot rice.

MAKES 8 SERVINGS

Pork Tenderloin Roast with Fig Sauce

Mustard Crusted Rib Roast

1 (3-rib) beef rib roast, trimmed* (6 to 7 pounds)

3 tablespoons Dijon mustard

1 tablespoon plus 1½ teaspoons chopped fresh tarragon *or* 1½ teaspoons dried tarragon

3 cloves garlic, minced

¼ cup dry red wine

⅓ cup finely chopped shallots (about 2 shallots)

1 tablespoon all-purpose flour

1 cup beef broth

Roasted red bell peppers and potatoes (optional)

Ask meat retailer to remove chine bone for easier carving. Trim fat to ¼-inch thickness.

1. Preheat oven to 450°F. Place roast, bone side down, in shallow roasting pan. Combine mustard, tarragon and garlic in small bowl; spread over all surfaces of roast except bottom. Insert meat thermometer into thickest part of roast, not touching bone or fat. Roast 10 minutes.

2. *Reduce oven temperature to 350°F.* Roast 2½ to 3 hours for medium or until internal temperature reaches 145°F.

3. Remove roast to large cutting board. Cover loosely with foil; let stand 10 to 15 minutes before carving into ½-inch-thick slices. Internal temperature will continue to rise 5° to 10°F during stand time.

4. To make gravy, pour drippings from roasting pan, reserving 1 tablespoon in medium saucepan. Add wine to roasting pan; place over two burners. Cook over medium heat 2 minutes or until slightly thickened, stirring to scrape up browned bits; set aside.

5. Add shallots to reserved drippings in saucepan; cook and stir over medium heat 4 minutes or until softened. Add flour; cook and stir 1 minute. Add broth and wine mixture; cook 5 minutes or until sauce thickens, stirring occasionally. Pour through strainer into gravy boat, pressing with back of spoon on shallots; discard solids. Serve sauce with roast, peppers and potatoes, if desired.

MAKES 6 TO 8 SERVINGS

Mustard Crusted Rib Roast

PLEASANT
POULTRY

Lemon Rosemary
Roasted Chicken & Potatoes

- 4 bone-in skin-on chicken breasts
- ½ cup lemon juice
- 6 tablespoons olive oil, divided
- 6 cloves garlic, minced and divided
- 2 tablespoons plus 1 teaspoon chopped fresh rosemary leaves *or* 2¼ teaspoons dried rosemary, divided
- 1½ teaspoons salt, divided
- 2 pounds small red potatoes, cut into quarters
- 1 large onion, cut into 2-inch pieces
- ¼ teaspoon black pepper

1. Place chicken in large resealable food storage bag. Combine lemon juice, 3 tablespoons oil, 3 cloves garlic, 1 tablespoon rosemary and ½ teaspoon salt in small bowl; pour over chicken. Seal bag; turn to coat. Refrigerate several hours or overnight.

2. Preheat oven to 400°F. Combine potatoes and onion in roasting pan. Combine remaining 3 tablespoons oil, 3 cloves garlic, 1 tablespoon rosemary, 1 teaspoon salt and pepper in small bowl; mix well. Pour over vegetables; toss to coat.

3. Drain chicken; discard marinade. Arrange chicken in pan with vegetables; sprinkle with remaining 1 teaspoon rosemary.

4. Roast 50 minutes or until chicken is cooked through (165°F) and potatoes are tender.

MAKES 4 SERVINGS

Lemon Rosemary Roasted Chicken & Potatoes

Turkey with Pecan-Cherry Stuffing

1 fresh or frozen boneless turkey breast (about 3 to 4 pounds)

2 cups cooked rice

⅓ cup chopped pecans

⅓ cup dried cherries or cranberries

1 teaspoon poultry seasoning

¼ cup peach, apricot or plum preserves

1 teaspoon Worcestershire sauce

Slow Cooker Directions

1. Thaw turkey breast, if frozen. Remove and discard skin. Cut slices three fourths of the way through turkey at 1-inch intervals.

2. Combine rice, pecans, cherries and poultry seasoning in large bowl; stir to blend. Stuff rice mixture between slices. (If necessary, skewer turkey lengthwise to hold it together.)

3. Place turkey in slow cooker. Cover; cook on LOW 5 to 6 hours or until turkey registers 170°F on meat thermometer inserted into thickest part of breast, not touching stuffing.

4. Combine preserves and Worcestershire sauce in small bowl; stir to blend. Spoon over turkey. Cover; let stand 5 minutes. If used, remove skewer before serving.

MAKES 8 SERVINGS

Serving Suggestion: Serve with asparagus spears.

Turkey with Pecan-Cherry Stuffing

Duck Breasts with Balsamic Honey Sauce

3   tablespoons balsamic vinegar
3   tablespoons honey
2   tablespoons lemon juice
4   boneless duck breasts (6 to 8 ounces each)
    Salt and black pepper
1   shallot, minced

1. Combine vinegar, honey and lemon juice in small bowl; mix well.

2. Score skin on duck breasts with tip of sharp knife in crosshatch pattern, being careful to cut only into the fat and not the meat. Season both sides with salt and pepper. Place duck breasts skin side down in large skillet over medium heat; cook 10 to 12 minutes or until skin is crisp and golden brown. Turn; cook 8 minutes or until medium rare (130°F). Remove duck to large plate; let stand 10 minutes before slicing.

3. Meanwhile, drain all but 1 tablespoon fat from skillet. Add shallot to skillet; cook and stir 2 to 3 minutes or until translucent. Add vinegar mixture; cook and stir 5 minutes or until slightly thickened. Slice duck; drizzle with sauce.

MAKES 4 SERVINGS

Herb-Roasted Chicken & Gravy

1   tub KNORR® Homestyle Stock–Chicken, divided
2   tablespoons chopped fresh herbs (fresh thyme leaves, tarragon and/or rosemary)
2   cloves garlic, chopped
3½   to 4-pound roasting chicken
1   cup water
2   tablespoons all-purpose flour

1. Preheat oven to 375°F.

2. Combine ½ tub KNORR® Homestyle Stock–Chicken, herbs and garlic in small bowl. Rub mixture under chicken skin, then spread remaining on outside of chicken. Arrange chicken on rack in roasting pan.

3. Roast chicken 2 hours or until meat thermometer inserted in thickest part of thigh reaches 165°F. Remove chicken from pan and keep warm.

4. To make gravy, combine water with flour in small bowl, then stir into pan over medium heat. Stir in remaining ½ tub Stock, scraping up brown bits from bottom of pan. Cook, stirring frequently, until gravy is slightly thickened, about 5 minutes. Strain, if desired. Serve gravy with chicken.

MAKES 8 SERVINGS

Duck Breasts with Balsamic Honey Sauce

Artichoke-Olive Chicken Bake

1½   cups uncooked rotini pasta
1   tablespoon olive oil
1   medium onion, chopped
½   green bell pepper, chopped
2   cups shredded cooked chicken
1   can (about 14 ounces) diced tomatoes with Italian herbs
1   can (14 ounces) artichoke hearts, drained and quartered
1   can (6 ounces) sliced black olives, drained
1   teaspoon Italian seasoning
2   cups (8 ounces) shredded mozzarella cheese

1. Preheat oven to 350°F. Spray 2-quart casserole with nonstick cooking spray. Cook pasta according to package directions; drain.

2. Heat oil in large skillet over medium heat. Add onion and bell pepper; cook and stir 1 minute. Add pasta, chicken, tomatoes, artichokes, olives and Italian seasoning; mix until blended.

3. Place half of chicken mixture in prepared casserole; sprinkle with half of cheese. Top with remaining chicken mixture and cheese.

4. Bake, covered, 35 minutes or until hot and bubbly.

MAKES 8 SERVINGS

Artichoke-Olive Chicken Bake

Java Coffee-Rubbed Roast Turkey

Rub

- ⅓ cup firmly packed dark brown sugar
- ⅓ cup medium-fine grind dark-roasted coffee
- 3 tablespoons ancho chili powder
- 2 tablespoons kosher salt
- 1 tablespoon black pepper
- 1 tablespoon unsweetened cocoa
- 2 teaspoons dried minced garlic
- 2 teaspoons smoked paprika
- ½ teaspoon ground cumin
- ½ teaspoon dry mustard

Turkey

- 1 (12- to 14-pound) BUTTERBALL® Fresh or Frozen Whole Turkey, thawed if frozen
  Vegetable oil

1. Combine brown sugar, coffee, chili powder, salt, pepper, cocoa, garlic, paprika, cumin and mustard in small bowl; mix well.

2. Remove neck and giblets from body and neck cavities of turkey. Refrigerate for another use or discard. Pat turkey dry with paper towels. Turn wings back to hold neck skin in place. Return legs to tucked position, if untucked. Place turkey, breast side up, on flat rack in shallow roasting pan. Brush breast and legs lightly with oil. Apply prepared rub on turkey skin; refrigerate 2 to 4 hours.

3. Preheat oven to 325°F. Roast turkey 1½ hours. Then, cover breast and top of drumsticks loosely with aluminum foil to prevent overcooking.

4. Continue roasting turkey 1½ to 2 hours* or until meat thermometer reaches 180°F when inserted into deepest part of thigh not touching bone.

5. Transfer turkey to cutting board; loosely tent with foil. Let stand 15 minutes before carving.

MAKES 10 TO 12 SERVINGS

Follow cooking times according to package directions; times vary with size of turkey.

Note: The Java Coffee Rub mixture can be stored in an airtight container in a cool, dry place for up to 3 weeks.

Java Coffee-Rubbed Roast Turkey

Spinach-Stuffed Chicken Breasts

4 boneless skinless chicken breasts (about 1 pound)

5 ounces frozen chopped spinach, thawed and squeezed dry

2 tablespoons freshly grated Parmesan cheese

1 teaspoon grated lemon peel, plus additional for garnish

¼ teaspoon black pepper

    Nonstick olive oil cooking spray

1 cup thinly sliced mushrooms

6 slices (2 ounces) thinly sliced ham

1 cup white grape juice

    Lemon wedges (optional)

1. Trim fat from chicken; discard. Place each chicken breast between two sheets of plastic wrap. Pound with meat mallet until chicken is about ¼ inch thick.

2. Preheat oven to 350°F. Pat spinach dry with paper towels. Combine spinach, cheese, 1 teaspoon lemon peel and black pepper in large bowl. Spray small nonstick skillet with cooking spray; heat over medium heat. Add mushrooms; cook and stir 3 to 4 minutes or until tender.

3. Arrange 1½ slices ham over each chicken breast. Spread each with one fourth of spinach mixture. Top each with mushrooms. Beginning with longer side, roll chicken tightly. Tie with kitchen string.

4. Place stuffed chicken breasts, seam side down, in 9-inch square baking pan. Lightly spray chicken with cooking spray. Pour white grape juice over top. Bake 30 minutes or until chicken is no longer pink.

5. Remove string; cut chicken rolls into ½-inch diagonal slices. Arrange on plate. Pour pan juices over chicken. Garnish with additional lemon peel and wedges.

MAKES 4 SERVINGS

Spinach-Stuffed Chicken Breasts

Roast Duck with Apple Stuffing

1 duck (about 5 pounds)
   Kosher salt and black pepper
2 tablespoons butter
1 small onion, chopped
2 stalks celery, chopped
3 apples, peeled and cut into bite-size pieces
½ cup chopped mixed dried fruit (prunes, apricots, etc.)
5 to 6 fresh sage leaves (tear large leaves in half)
1 cup dried bread cubes (¼- to ½-inch pieces)
   Juice of 1 lemon
1 cup plus 1 tablespoon chicken broth, divided
⅔ cup dry white wine

1. Discard neck, giblets and liver from duck (or reserve for another use); trim fat. Rinse duck thoroughly; pat dry with paper towels. Generously season outside of duck and cavity with salt and pepper. Place duck on rack in roasting pan. Refrigerate, uncovered, 1 to 3 hours until ready to cook.

2. Melt butter in medium skillet over medium-high heat. Add onion and celery; cook and stir 2 minutes. Add apples, dried fruit and sage; cook and stir 10 minutes or until apples and vegetables are softened. Combine apple mixture and bread cubes in medium bowl; season with ½ teaspoon salt and ¼ teaspoon pepper. Stir in lemon juice. If stuffing seems dry, add 1 tablespoon broth.

3. Preheat oven to 350°F. Spoon stuffing into duck cavity, packing tightly. Tie legs together with kitchen string. Cut through duck skin in crisscross pattern over breast and legs, being careful to only cut through skin and fat layer (about ¼ inch thick), but not into duck flesh. (Cuts will help render duck fat and make skin crisp.)

4. Roast 1½ to 2 hours or until juices run clear and thermometer inserted into leg joint registers 175°F, rotating pan every 20 minutes. (Temperature of stuffing should reach 165°F.) Remove duck to large cutting board.

5. Pour off fat from pan; discard. Heat roasting pan over medium-high heat. Add wine; cook and stir 5 minutes or until wine is reduced by half, scraping up browned bits from bottom of pan. Add remaining 1 cup broth; cook and stir 2 minutes. Strain sauce; serve with duck and stuffing.

MAKES 4 SERVINGS

Tip: Ducks' looks are deceiving—they are large birds, but have very little meat for their size. One duck can serve four, provided there are side dishes (and all four people don't want a duck leg!) For a bigger group, double the stuffing recipe and roast two ducks.

Roast Duck with Apple Stuffing

Saffron Chicken & Vegetables

2   tablespoons vegetable oil

6   bone-in skinless chicken thighs

1   bag (16 ounces) frozen mixed vegetables, such as broccoli, red bell peppers, mushrooms and onions, thawed

1   can (about 14 ounces) chicken broth

1   can (10¾ ounces) condensed cream of chicken soup, undiluted

1   can (10¾ ounces) condensed cream of mushroom soup, undiluted

1   package (8 ounces) saffron yellow rice mix

½   cup water

1   teaspoon paprika (optional)

1. Preheat oven to 350°F. Spray 3-quart casserole with nonstick cooking spray.

2. Heat oil in large skillet over medium heat. Add chicken; cook 5 to 7 minutes or until browned on both sides. Drain fat.

3. Meanwhile, combine vegetables, broth, soups, rice mix and water in large bowl; mix well. Place mixture in prepared casserole. Top with chicken. Sprinkle with paprika, if desired. Cover; bake 1½ hours or until chicken is cooked through (165°F).

MAKES 6 SERVINGS

Turkey Stuffing Bake

1¾   cups SWANSON® Chicken Stock

Generous dash ground black pepper

1   stalk celery, chopped (about ½ cup)

1   small onion, coarsely chopped (about ¼ cup)

4   cups PEPPERIDGE FARM® Herb Seasoned Stuffing

12   ounces sliced cooked turkey

1   jar (12 ounces) CAMPBELL'S® Slow Roast Turkey Gravy

1. Heat the stock, black pepper, celery and onion in a 3-quart saucepan over medium-high heat to a boil. Reduce the heat to low. Cover and cook for 5 minutes or until the vegetables are tender. Remove the saucepan from the heat. Add the stuffing to the saucepan and mix lightly.

2. Spoon the stuffing mixture into a 2-quart shallow baking dish. Arrange the turkey over the stuffing. Pour the gravy over the turkey.

3. Bake at 350°F. for 30 minutes or until the turkey and stuffing are hot.

MAKES 4 SERVINGS

Saffron Chicken & Vegetables

Roast Capon with Fruit and Nut Stuffing

4	tablespoons butter, divided
1	tart apple, diced
½	cup chopped golden raisins or dried cranberries
¼	cup sliced green onions
¼	cup chopped celery
4	cups stale bread cubes
2	tablespoons chopped fresh parsley *or* 1 teaspoon dried parsley
2	teaspoons poultry seasoning
1	teaspoon salt
½	teaspoon black pepper
1½	cups chicken broth
½	cup dry sherry
½	cup slivered almonds, toasted*
¼	cup honey
2	tablespoons prepared mustard
½	teaspoon curry powder
1	capon (8 to 9 pounds)
¼	cup water
¼	cup all-purpose flour

To toast almonds, spread in single layer on baking sheet. Bake in preheated 350°F oven 5 to 7 minutes or until lightly toasted, stirring occasionally.

1. Preheat oven to 325°F.

2. Melt 2 tablespoons butter in skillet over medium-high heat. Add apple, raisins, green onions and celery; cook and stir 3 minutes or until fruit is tender. Add bread cubes; toss. Add parsley, poultry seasoning, salt and pepper; toss. Add broth, sherry and almonds; toss until combined.

3. Bring honey, remaining 2 tablespoons butter, mustard and curry powder to a boil in saucepan over medium-high heat. Boil 1 minute; remove from heat.

4. Remove giblets and neck from capon; reserve for another use. Rinse capon under cold water and pat dry with paper towels. Stuff cavity loosely with about 3 cups stuffing (place remaining stuffing in greased baking dish). Tie legs together with wet cotton string and place, breast side up, on rack in shallow roasting pan coated with nonstick cooking spray. Insert meat thermometer into meaty part of thigh not touching bone.

5. Bake 3 hours or until meat thermometer registers 170°F, brushing well with glaze every 30 minutes. Loosely cover remaining stuffing. Place in oven during last 45 minutes of baking time.

6. Remove capon to large serving platter. Remove stuffing from cavity and add to remaining stuffing. Cover capon with foil; let stand 10 minutes before carving.

7. Strain roasting pan juices into 2-cup glass measure; skim off fat. Add enough water to pan juices to equal 2 cups. Pour pan juice mixture into saucepan and place over medium heat. Combine ¼ cup water and flour in small bowl; stir until smooth. Gradually whisk flour mixture into saucepan; bring to a boil. Reduce heat to medium-low; simmer 2 to 3 minutes or until thickened. Serve with capon and stuffing.

MAKES 8 SERVINGS

Chicken Mirabella

- 4   boneless skinless chicken breasts (about 4 ounces each)
- ½   cup pitted prunes
- ½   cup assorted pitted olives (black, green and/or combination)
- ¼   cup dry white wine
- 2   tablespoons olive oil
- 1   tablespoon capers
- 1   tablespoon red wine vinegar
- 1   teaspoon dried oregano
- 1   clove garlic, minced
- ½   teaspoon chopped fresh parsley, plus additional for garnish
- 2   teaspoons packed brown sugar

1. Preheat oven to 350°F.

2. Place chicken in 8-inch baking dish. Combine prunes, olives, wine, oil, capers, vinegar, oregano, garlic and ½ teaspoon parsley in medium bowl; stir to blend. Pour evenly over chicken. Sprinkle with brown sugar.

3. Bake 25 to 30 minutes or until no longer pink in center, basting with sauce halfway through. Garnish with additional parsley.

MAKES 4 SERVINGS

Tip: For more intense flavor, marinate chicken at least 8 hours or overnight and sprinkle with brown sugar just before baking.

Serving Suggestion: Serve with long grain and wild rice.

Herb Roasted Turkey

½ cup coarse-grain or Dijon mustard
¼ cup chopped fresh sage
2 tablespoons chopped fresh thyme
2 tablespoons chopped fresh chives
1 small (8- to 10-pound) turkey, thawed if frozen
   Salt and black pepper

1. Preheat oven to 450°F. Combine mustard, sage, thyme and chives in small bowl; mix well.

2. Rinse turkey under cold water; pat dry with paper towels. Carefully insert fingers under skin, beginning at neck cavity and sliding down over breast to form pocket between skin and turkey breast. Spoon mustard mixture into pocket; massage outside of skin to spread mixture into even layer.

3. Place turkey, breast side up, on rack in shallow roasting pan. Tie legs together with kitchen string. Season with salt and pepper.

4. Place turkey in oven. *Reduce oven temperature to 325°F.* Roast turkey 18 minutes per pound or until cooked through (165°F). Once turkey browns, tent with foil for remainder of roasting time. Remove turkey to large cutting board; reserve pan drippings for gravy, if desired. Loosely tent turkey with foil; let stand 20 minutes before carving.

MAKES 8 TO 10 SERVINGS

Harvest Chicken

1 can (10¾ ounces) reduced-fat condensed cream of chicken soup, undiluted
½ cup milk
¾ teaspoon Italian seasoning
¼ teaspoon dried thyme
   Nonstick cooking spray
4 boneless skinless chicken breasts
2 medium red or green apples, cored and sliced
1 small onion, thinly sliced into rings

1. Combine soup, milk, Italian seasoning and thyme in small bowl; set aside.

2. Spray large nonstick skillet with cooking spray; heat over medium heat 1 minute. Add chicken; cook 5 minutes on each side or until browned. Remove from skillet; set aside.

3. Add apples and onion to skillet; cook 4 to 6 minutes or until onion is tender. Stir in reserved soup mixture and chicken. Reduce heat to low. Cover; simmer 5 to 10 minutes or until chicken is no longer pink in center.

MAKES 4 SERVINGS

Herb Roasted Turkey

Chicken & Broccoli with Garlic Sauce

    1   tablespoon olive oil
    4   boneless, skinless chicken breast halves (about 1¼ pounds)
    1   package (10 ounces) frozen broccoli florets, thawed
    1   envelope LIPTON® RECIPE SECRETS® Savory Herb with Garlic Soup Mix
    ¾   cup water
    1   teaspoon soy sauce

1. In 12-inch nonstick skillet, heat oil over medium-high heat and brown chicken. Remove chicken and set aside.

2. In same skillet, add broccoli and soup mix blended with water and soy sauce. Bring to a boil over high heat.

3. Return chicken to skillet. Reduce heat to low and simmer covered 10 minutes or until chicken is thoroughly cooked. Serve, if desired, over hot cooked rice.

MAKES 4 SERVINGS

Swiss Melt Chicken

    1   tablespoon olive oil
    ¼   cup minced onion
    1   clove garlic, minced
    4   boneless skinless chicken breasts
    1   package (about 6 ounces) long grain and wild rice
    1⅔   cups chicken broth
    1   cup sliced mushrooms
    ½   cup chopped green bell pepper
    ½   cup chopped red bell pepper
    4   slices Swiss cheese

1. Heat oil in large skillet over medium heat. Add onion and garlic; cook and stir 2 minutes or until onion is soft. Add chicken; cook 5 to 7 minutes until light brown, turning once. Add rice, contents of seasoning packet and broth. Bring to a boil. Cover; simmer 20 minutes or until rice is tender.

2. Stir in mushrooms and bell peppers; cook, covered, 5 to 8 minutes or until chicken is no longer pink in center. Place cheese over chicken; remove from heat. Let stand, covered, 5 minutes or until cheese is melted.

MAKES 4 SERVINGS

Chicken & Broccoli with Garlic Sauce

Duck Breast with
Cherry Sauce & Sweet Potato Pancakes

Sweet Potato Pancakes

- 2 sweet potatoes, peeled
- 1 russet potato, peeled
- ½ cup all-purpose flour
- ⅓ cup minced green onions
- 2 eggs, lightly beaten
- ½ teaspoon salt
- ½ teaspoon black pepper
- ¼ teaspoon ground nutmeg
- Vegetable oil

Cherry Sauce

- 1 cup dry red wine
- 1 cup sour cherry preserves
- ½ cup dried cherries
- 4 tablespoons red wine vinegar

Duck

- 4 boneless duck breasts (about 2 pounds)

Sweet Potato Pancakes

1. Attach slicer/shredder to stand mixer with coarse shredding blade. Shred sweet potatoes into mixing bowl. Squeeze as much moisture as possible out of shredded potatoes in colander or strainer.

2. Return potatoes to mixing bowl. Add flour, green onions, egg, salt, pepper and nutmeg; mix until combined. Heat ¼-inch oil in large skillet over medium-high heat. Pat handfuls of potato mixture into cakes about 3 inches in diameter. Cook without crowding pan 3 to 5 minutes per side until firm and browned around edge. Keep warm.

Cherry Sauce

3. Meanwhile, soak dried cherries in wine in small bowl 15 minutes or until plump. Combine wine, cherries, cherry preserves and vinegar in small saucepan. Simmer gently 10 minutes or until ready to serve.

Duck

4. Place duck breast, skin side up, on cutting board. Cut criss cross lines through skin and fat layer only. Cook, skin side down, in large skillet over medium heat 5 minutes or until fat is rendered and skin is browned, pouring off excess fat as needed. Turn over; cook 5 minutes or until duck is browned but still pink in center. Slice and keep warm.

5. Arrange duck and sweet potato pancakes on serving dishes. Top with Cherry Sauce.

MAKES 4 SERVINGS

Duck Breast with Cherry Sauce
& Sweet Potato Pancakes

Crispy Roasted Chicken

1   roasting chicken or capon (about 6½ pounds)
1   tablespoon peanut or vegetable oil
2   cloves garlic, minced
1   tablespoon soy sauce

1. Preheat oven to 350°F. Place chicken on rack in shallow, foil-lined roasting pan.

2. Combine oil and garlic in small cup; brush evenly over chicken. Roast 15 to 20 minutes per pound or until internal temperature reaches 170°F when tested with meat thermometer inserted in thickest part of thigh not touching bone.

3. *Increase oven temperature to 450°F.* Remove drippings from pan; discard. Brush chicken evenly with soy sauce. Roast 5 to 10 minutes until skin is crisp and golden brown. Remove chicken to large cutting board; let stand 10 to 15 minutes before carving. Internal temperature will continue to rise 5° to 10°F during stand time. Cover; refrigerate leftovers up to three days or freeze up to three months.

MAKES 8 TO 10 SERVINGS

Turkey 'n' Stuffing Pie

1¼ cups water*
¼ cup butter or margarine*
3½ cups seasoned stuffing crumbs*
1⅓ cups FRENCH'S® French Fried Onions
1½ cups (7 ounces) cubed cooked turkey
1   can (10¾ ounces) condensed cream of celery soup
1   package (10 ounces) frozen peas, thawed and drained
¾ cup milk

Three cups leftover stuffing can be substituted for water, butter and stuffing crumbs. If stuffing is dry, stir in water, 1 tablespoon at a time, until moist but not wet.

Preheat oven to 350°F. In medium saucepan, heat water and butter; stir until butter melts. Remove from heat. Stir in seasoned stuffing crumbs and ⅔ *cup* French Fried Onions. Spoon stuffing mixture into 9-inch round or fluted baking dish. Press stuffing evenly across bottom and up sides of dish to form a shell. In medium bowl, combine turkey, soup, peas and milk; pour into stuffing shell. Bake, covered, at 350°F for 30 minutes or until heated through. Top with remaining ⅔ *cup* onions; bake, uncovered, 5 minutes or until onions are golden brown.

MAKES 4 TO 6 SERVINGS

Crispy Roasted Chicken

Crispy Duck

1 whole duck (about 5 pounds)
1 tablespoon rubbed sage
1 teaspoon salt
¼ teaspoon black pepper
3 cups vegetable oil
1 tablespoon butter
2 large Granny Smith or Rome Beauty apples, cored and cut into thin wedges
½ cup clover honey

1. Remove neck and giblets from duck. Cut wing tips and second wing sections off duck; wrap and freeze for another use. Trim excess fat and excess skin from duck; discard. Rinse duck and cavity under cold running water; pat dry with paper towels. Cut duck into quarters, removing backbone and breast bone.

2. Place duck in 13×9-inch baking dish. Combine sage, salt and pepper. Rub duck with sage mixture. Cover; refrigerate 1 hour.

3. To steam duck, place wire rack in wok. Add water to 1 inch below rack. (Water should not touch rack.) Cover wok; bring water to a boil over medium-high heat. Arrange duck, skin sides up, on wire rack. Cover; steam 40 minutes or until fork-tender. (Add boiling water to wok to keep water at same level.)

4. Remove cooked duck to plate. Carefully remove rack from wok; discard water. Rinse wok and dry. Heat oil in wok over medium-high heat until oil registers 375°F on deep-fry thermometer. Add half of duck, skin sides down. Fry 5 to 10 minutes or until crisp and golden brown, turning once. Drain duck on paper towels. Repeat with remaining duck, reheating oil.

5. Pour off oil. Melt butter in wok over medium heat. Add apples; cook and stir 5 minutes or until wilted. Stir in honey and bring to a boil. Transfer apples with slotted spoon to warm serving platter. Arrange duck on apples. Drizzle honey mixture over duck.

MAKES 4 SERVINGS

Quick Chicken Pot Pie

1 pound boneless skinless chicken thighs, cut into 1-inch cubes

1 can (about 14 ounces) chicken broth

3 tablespoons all-purpose flour

2 tablespoons butter, softened

1 package (10 ounces) frozen mixed vegetables, thawed

1 can (about 4 ounces) button mushrooms, drained

¼ teaspoon dried basil

¼ teaspoon dried oregano

¼ teaspoon dried thyme

1 cup biscuit baking mix

6 tablespoons milk

1. Preheat oven to 450°F.

2. Place chicken and broth in large skillet; cover and bring to a boil over high heat. Reduce heat to medium; simmer, uncovered, 5 minutes or until chicken is tender.

3. Mix flour and butter; set aside. Combine mixed vegetables, mushrooms, basil, oregano and thyme in greased 2-quart casserole.

4. Add flour mixture to chicken and broth in skillet; cook and stir until smooth and thickened. Add to vegetable mixture; mix well.

5. Blend biscuit mix and milk in medium bowl until smooth. Drop four scoops batter onto chicken mixture. Bake 18 to 20 minutes or until biscuits are browned and casserole is hot and bubbly.

MAKES 4 SERVINGS

 tip

This dish can be prepared through step 4 covered and refrigerated up to 24 hours, if desired, proceed with step 4. Bake as directed 20 to 25 minutes.

Spicy Buttermilk Oven-Fried Chicken

3½ pounds whole chicken, cut up
2 cups buttermilk
1½ cups all-purpose flour
1 teaspoon salt
1 teaspoon ground red pepper
½ teaspoon garlic powder
¼ cup canola oil

1. Place chicken pieces in single layer in 13×9-inch baking dish. Pour buttermilk over chicken. Cover with plastic wrap and refrigerate; let marinate at least 2 hours.

2. Preheat oven to 350°F. Combine flour, salt, red pepper and garlic powder in large shallow bowl. Heat oil in large skillet over medium-high heat.

3. Remove chicken pieces from buttermilk; coat with flour mixture. Place chicken in hot oil; cook 10 minutes or until brown and crisp on all sides. Place chicken in single layer in 13×9-inch baking dish. Bake, uncovered, 30 to 45 minutes or until chicken is cooked through (165°F).

MAKES 6 SERVINGS

Turkey and Biscuits

2 cans (10¾ ounces each) condensed cream of chicken soup
¼ cup dry white wine
¼ teaspoon poultry seasoning
2 packages (8 ounces each) frozen chopped asparagus, thawed
3 cups cubed cooked turkey or chicken
   Paprika (optional)
1 can (11 ounces) refrigerated flaky biscuit dough

1. Preheat oven to 350°F. Spray 13×9-inch baking dish with nonstick cooking spray.

2. Combine soup, wine and poultry seasoning in medium bowl. Arrange asparagus in single layer in prepared dish. Place turkey evenly over asparagus. Spread soup mixture over turkey. Sprinkle lightly with paprika, if desired.

3. Cover tightly with foil and bake 20 minutes. Remove from oven. *Increase oven temperature to 425°F.* Top with biscuit dough and bake, uncovered, 8 to 10 minutes or until biscuits are golden brown.

MAKES 6 SERVINGS

Spicy Buttermilk Oven-Fried Chicken

Herbed Turkey Breast with Orange Sauce

1 large onion, chopped

3 cloves garlic, minced

1 teaspoon dried rosemary

½ teaspoon black pepper

1 boneless skinless turkey breast (3 pounds)

1½ cups orange juice

Slow Cooker Directions

1. Place onion in slow cooker. Combine garlic, rosemary and pepper in small bowl; set aside. Cut slices about three-fourths of the way through turkey at 2-inch intervals. Rub garlic mixture between slices.

2. Place turkey, cut side up, in slow cooker. Pour orange juice over turkey. Cover; cook on LOW 7 to 8 hours. Serve sauce from slow cooker with sliced turkey.

MAKES 6 SERVINGS

Orange-Ginger Broiled Cornish Hens

2 large Cornish hens, split (about 1½ pounds each)

2 teaspoons peanut or vegetable oil, divided

¼ cup orange marmalade

1 tablespoon minced fresh ginger

1. Place hens, skin side up, on rack of foil-lined broiler pan. Brush with 1 teaspoon oil.

2. Broil 6 to 7 inches from heat 10 minutes. Turn hens skin side down; brush with remaining 1 teaspoon oil. Broil 10 minutes.

3. Combine marmalade and ginger in cup; brush half of mixture over hens. Broil 5 minutes.

4. Turn hens skin side up; brush with remaining marmalade mixture. Broil 5 minutes or until juices run clear (180°F) and hens are browned and glazed.

MAKES 4 SERVINGS

Herbed Turkey Breast with Orange Sauce

Garlic 'n Lemon Roast Chicken

1 small onion, finely chopped
1 envelope LIPTON® RECIPE SECRETS® Savory Herb with Garlic Soup Mix
2 tablespoons olive oil
2 tablespoons lemon juice
1 (3½-pound) roasting chicken

1. In large plastic bag or bowl, combine onion and soup mix blended with oil and lemon juice; add chicken. Close bag and shake, or toss in bowl, until chicken is evenly coated. Cover and marinate in refrigerator, turning occasionally, 2 hours.

2. Preheat oven to 350°F. Place chicken and marinade in 13×9-inch baking or roasting pan. Arrange chicken, breast side up; discard bag.

3. Bake uncovered, basting occasionally, 1 hour and 20 minutes or until meat thermometer reaches 180°F. (Insert meat thermometer into thickest part of thigh between breast and thigh; make sure tip does not touch bone.)

MAKES 4 SERVINGS

Orange-Glazed Chicken

1 teaspoon salt
½ teaspoon black pepper
1 broiler-fryer chicken (2½ to 3 pounds), cut in half
½ cup orange marmalade
3 tablespoons butter
1 tablespoon dried onion flakes
1 clove garlic, minced
¼ teaspoon dried thyme
 Orange wedges (optional)
 Fresh parsley or cilantro (optional)

1. Combine salt and pepper; rub over chicken. Arrange chicken, breast side up, in 13×9-inch baking pan. Bake, uncovered, 30 minutes.

2. Heat medium saucepan over medium heat. Add marmalade, butter, onion flakes, garlic and thyme; cook and stir 1 to 2 minutes. Baste chicken with marmalade mixture two to three times.

3. Bake, uncovered, 15 to 20 minutes or until chicken is no longer pink in center and juices run clear. Remove from oven. Discard remaining marmalade mixture. Garnish with orange wedges and parsley.

MAKES 4 TO 6 SERVINGS

Garlic 'n Lemon Roast Chicken

Turkey Breast with Barley-Cranberry Stuffing

2	cups chicken broth
1	cup uncooked quick-cooking barley
½	cup chopped onion
½	cup dried cranberries
2	tablespoons slivered almonds, toasted*
½	teaspoon rubbed sage
½	teaspoon garlic-pepper seasoning
	Nonstick cooking spray
1	fresh or thawed frozen bone-in turkey breast half (about 2 pounds), skinned
⅓	cup finely chopped fresh parsley

To toast almonds, spread in single layer in heavy skillet. Cook over medium heat 1 to 2 minutes or until nuts are lightly browned, stirring frequently.

Slow Cooker Directions

1. Combine broth, barley, onion, cranberries, almonds, sage and garlic-pepper seasoning in slow cooker.

2. Spray large nonstick skillet with cooking spray; heat over medium heat. Add turkey breast; cook 6 to 8 minutes or until browned on all sides. Remove to slow cooker. Cover; cook on LOW 4 to 6 hours.

3. Remove turkey to large cutting board. Cover with foil; let stand 10 to 15 minutes before slicing. Stir parsley into sauce mixture in slow cooker. Serve sliced turkey with sauce and stuffing.

MAKES 6 SERVINGS

Turkey Breast with Barley-Cranberry Stuffing

Chicken Zucchini Casserole

1 package (about 6 ounces) herb-flavored stuffing mix

½ cup (1 stick) butter, melted

2 cups cubed zucchini

1½ cups chopped cooked chicken

1 can (10¾ ounces) condensed cream of celery soup, undiluted

1 cup grated carrots

1 onion, chopped

½ cup sour cream

½ cup (2 ounces) shredded Cheddar cheese

1. Preheat oven to 350°F. Combine stuffing mix and butter in medium bowl; reserve 1 cup stuffing. Place remaining stuffing in 13×9-inch baking dish.

2. Combine zucchini, chicken, soup, carrots, onion and sour cream in large bowl; mix well. Pour over stuffing in baking dish; top with reserved 1 cup stuffing and cheese.

3. Bake 40 to 45 minutes or until heated through and cheese is melted.

MAKES 8 SERVINGS

Chicken Zucchini Casserole

Roast Turkey with Pan Gravy

1 fresh or thawed frozen turkey (12 to 14 pounds), giblets and neck reserved (discard liver or reserve for another use)

Prepared stuffing

2 cloves garlic, minced

½ cup (1 stick) butter, melted

Turkey Broth with Giblets (recipe follows)

1 cup dry white wine or vermouth

3 tablespoons all-purpose flour

Salt and black pepper

1. Preheat oven to 450°F.

2. Rinse turkey; pat dry with paper towels. Stuff body and neck cavities loosely with stuffing. Fold skin over openings and close with skewers. Tie legs together with cotton string. Tuck wings under turkey. Place turkey on meat rack in shallow roasting pan. Stir garlic into butter. Insert ovenproof meat thermometer into thickest part of thigh not touching bone. Brush ⅓ of butter mixture evenly over turkey. Place turkey in oven. *Reduce oven temperature to 325°F.*

3. Roast 22 to 24 minutes per pound, brushing with butter mixture after 1 hour and then after 1½ hours. Baste with pan juices every hour of roasting. (Total roasting time should be 4 to 5 hours.) If turkey is overbrowning, tent with foil. Roast until internal temperature reaches 180°F when tested with meat thermometer inserted into the thickest part of thigh, not touching bone.

4. Meanwhile, prepare Turkey Broth with Giblets.

5. Remove turkey to large cutting board; tent with foil. Let stand 15 minutes. Pour off and reserve juices from roasting pan. To deglaze pan, pour wine into pan. Place over burners and cook over medium-high heat; scrape up browned bits and stir constantly 2 to 3 minutes or until mixture is reduced by about half.

6. Reserve ⅓ cup fat from pan drippings; discard remaining fat.* Place ⅓ cup fat in large saucepan. Add flour; cook and stir over medium heat 1 minute.

7. Slowly stir in 3 cups Turkey Broth, reserved pan juices and deglazed wine mixture from roasting pan. Cook over medium heat 10 minutes, stirring occasionally. Stir in reserved chopped giblets; heat through. Season with salt and pepper.

MAKES 12 SERVINGS AND 3½ CUPS GRAVY

Or, substitute ⅓ cup butter for turkey fat.

Turkey Broth with Giblets

  Reserved giblets and neck from turkey
 4 cups water
 1 can (about 14 ounces) chicken broth
 1 cup whipping cream (optional)
 1 medium onion, cut into quarters
 2 medium carrots, coarsely chopped
 4 large sprigs fresh parsley
 1 bay leaf
 1 teaspoon dried thyme, crushed
10 whole black peppercorns

1. Combine giblets and neck, water, broth and cream, if desired, in large saucepan. Bring to a boil over high heat; skim off foam. Stir in onion, carrots, parsley, bay leaf, thyme and peppercorns. Reduce heat to low. Simmer, uncovered, 1½ to 2 hours, stirring occasionally. (If liquid evaporates too quickly, add additional ½ cup water.) Cool to room temperature.

2. Strain broth; set aside. If broth measures less than 3 cups, add water to equal 3 cups liquid. If broth measures more than 3 cups, bring to a boil and heat until liquid is reduced to 3 cups. Remove meat from neck and chop giblets finely; set aside. Broth may be prepared up to one day before serving. Cover giblets and broth separately and refrigerate.

MAKES 3 CUPS

Chicken & Goat Cheese Rolls

4 boneless skinless chicken breasts
Salt and black pepper
½ cup basil-flavored goat cheese
¼ cup chopped drained sun-dried tomatoes, packed in oil
1 tablespoon olive oil

1. Preheat oven to 350°F. Place chicken on cutting board. Cover with plastic wrap. Pound with flat side of meat mallet to ¼-inch thickness. Remove plastic wrap. Season with salt and black pepper.

2. Combine goat cheese and tomatoes in small bowl; mix well. Spread goat cheese mixture onto chicken to within ½ inch of edges. Roll up chicken breasts, beginning with short edges, tucking ends in. Secure with toothpicks.

3. Heat oil in medium skillet over medium heat. Add chicken rolls; cook 6 to 8 minutes or until browned on all sides. Transfer rolls to baking sheet. Bake 15 minutes or until cooked through. Cut rolls diagonally into slices.

MAKES 4 SERVINGS

Serving Suggestion: Serve chicken rolls with pasta sauce.

Chicken & Goat Cheese Rolls

Yuletide
DESSERTS

Luscious Pecan Bread Pudding

  3 cups day-old French bread cubes
  3 tablespoons chopped pecans, toasted*
2¼ cups milk
  2 eggs, lightly beaten
  ½ cup sugar
  1 teaspoon vanilla
  ¾ teaspoon ground cinnamon, divided
  ¾ cup cranberry juice cocktail
1½ cups frozen pitted tart cherries
  2 tablespoons sugar

To toast pecans, spread in single layer in heavy-bottomed skillet. Cook over medium heat 1 to 2 minutes, stirring frequently, until nuts are lightly browned. Remove from skillet immediately. Cool before using.

Slow Cooker Directions

1. Toss bread cubes and pecans in soufflé dish. Combine milk, eggs, sugar, vanilla and ½ teaspoon cinnamon in large bowl. Pour over bread mixture in soufflé dish. Cover tightly with foil. Make foil handles (see Note). Place soufflé dish in slow cooker. Pour hot water into slow cooker to about 1½ inches from top of soufflé dish. Cover; cook on LOW 2 to 3 hours.

2. Meanwhile, combine cranberry juice and remaining ¼ teaspoon cinnamon in small saucepan; stir in frozen cherries. Bring sauce to a boil over medium heat; cook about 5 minutes. Remove from heat. Stir in sugar.

3. Lift soufflé dish from slow cooker with foil handles. Serve bread pudding with cherry sauce.

MAKES 6 SERVINGS

Note: Tear off three 18×2-inch strips of heavy foil or use regular foil folded to double thickness. Crisscross foil strips in spoke design and place in slow cooker to allow for easy removal of bread pudding.

Luscious Pecan Bread Pudding

Pear & Cranberry Strudel
with Caramel Sauce

½   of a 17.3-ounce package PEPPERIDGE FARM® Puff Pastry Sheets (1 sheet)

1   egg

1   tablespoon water

½   cup dried cranberries

½   cup packed brown sugar

2   tablespoons cornstarch

½   teaspoon ground cinnamon

2   large Bosc pears, peeled, cored and diced

¾   cup prepared caramel topping

1. Thaw the pastry sheet at room temperature for 40 minutes or until it's easy to handle. Heat the oven to 375°F. Lightly grease or line a baking sheet with parchment paper. Beat the egg and water in a small bowl with a fork.

2. Place the cranberries into a small bowl and pour hot water over them to cover. Let stand for 5 minutes. Drain. Mix the brown sugar, cornstarch and cinnamon in a medium bowl. Add the pears and cranberries and toss to coat.

3. Unroll the pastry sheet on a lightly floured surface. Roll the pastry sheet into a 14×11-inch rectangle. With the long side facing you, spoon the pear mixture onto the lower third of the pastry. Starting at the long side, roll up like a jelly roll. Tuck the ends under to seal. Place seam-side down on the baking sheet. Brush with the egg mixture. Cut several 2-inch-long slits 2 inches apart on the top.

4. Bake for 25 minutes or until the strudel is golden. Cool on the baking sheet on a wire rack for 15 minutes. Heat the caramel topping according to the package directions and serve with the strudel.

MAKES 6 SERVINGS

Kitchen Tip: Prepare the strudel through Step 3 and refrigerate for up to 24 hours or freeze.

Pear & Cranberry Strudel with Caramel Sauce

Old-Fashioned Caramel & Candied Bacon Apples

Candied Bacon (recipe follows), crumbled
1 package (14 ounces) caramels
2 tablespoons water
6 wooden craft sticks
6 medium Granny Smith apples

1. Prepare Candied Bacon.

2. Place caramels and water in medium heavy saucepan. Cook, stirring frequently, over medium-low heat until melted and very hot.

3. Insert stick into stem end of each apple. Place crumbled bacon in shallow bowl. Dip apple into caramel, tilting saucepan until apple is coated. Let excess caramel drip back into saucepan. Remove excess caramel by scraping bottom of apple across rim of saucepan.

4. Immediately roll apple in crumbled bacon. Place, stick side up, on baking sheet lined with waxed paper. Repeat with remaining apples. Rewarm caramel, if needed. Refrigerate at least 10 minutes or until caramel is firm.

MAKES 6 APPLES

Candied Bacon

4 to 6 slices thick-cut bacon
¼ to ½ cup packed brown sugar

Preheat oven to 400°F. Line 15×10-inch jelly-roll pan with heavy-duty foil. Coat both sides of each strip of bacon with brown sugar. Bake 18 to 20 minutes or until crispy, turning halfway through cooking time.

Old-Fashioned Caramel & Candied Bacon Apples

Creamy Chocolate Pudding

6 tablespoons granulated sugar

¼ cup NESTLÉ® TOLL HOUSE® Baking Cocoa

¼ cup cornstarch

⅛ teaspoon salt

1 can (12 fluid ounces) NESTLÉ® CARNATION® Evaporated Fat Free Milk

½ cup water

1 tablespoon butter or margarine

½ teaspoon vanilla extract

COMBINE sugar, cocoa, cornstarch and salt in medium saucepan. Add evaporated milk and water; whisk to blend.

COOK over medium heat, stirring constantly, for about 7 minutes or until pudding thickens. Do not boil. Remove from heat; stir in butter and vanilla extract.

MAKES ABOUT 4 SERVINGS

Cran-Raspberry Hazelnut Trifle

2 cups hazelnut-flavored liquid dairy creamer

1 package (3.4 ounces) instant vanilla pudding and pie filling mix

1 package (about 11 ounces) frozen pound cake, thawed

1 can (21 ounces) raspberry pie filling

1 can (16 ounces) whole berry cranberry sauce

Whipped topping, fresh raspberries and sprigs fresh mint (optional)

1. Combine creamer and pudding mix in medium bowl; beat with wire whisk 1 to 2 minutes or until thickened.

2. Cut pound cake into ¾-inch cubes. Combine pie filling and cranberry sauce in another medium bowl; blend well.

3. Layer one third of cake cubes, one third of fruit sauce and one third of pudding mixture in 1½- to 2-quart straight-sided glass serving bowl. Repeat layers twice. Cover; refrigerate until serving time. Garnish with whipped topping, fresh raspberries and mint.

MAKES 8 SERVINGS

Creamy Chocolate Pudding

Pumpkin Custard

1 cup solid-pack pumpkin
½ cup packed brown sugar
2 eggs, beaten
½ teaspoon ground ginger
½ teaspoon grated lemon peel
½ teaspoon ground cinnamon, plus additional for garnish
1 can (12 ounces) evaporated milk

Slow Cooker Directions

1. Combine pumpkin, brown sugar, eggs, ginger, lemon peel and ½ teaspoon cinnamon in large bowl. Stir in evaporated milk. Divide mixture among six ramekins or custard cups. Cover each cup tightly with foil.

2. Place ramekins in slow cooker. Pour water into slow cooker to come about ½ inch from top of ramekins. Cover; cook on LOW 4 hours.

3. Use tongs or slotted spoon to remove ramekins from slow cooker. Sprinkle with additional ground cinnamon. Serve warm.

MAKES 6 SERVINGS

Mocha Nog

1 quart eggnog
1 tablespoon instant French vanilla or regular coffee granules
¼ cup coffee-flavored liqueur
Whipped cream (optional)

1. Heat eggnog and coffee granules in large saucepan over medium heat until mixture is heated through and coffee granules are dissolved. *Do not boil.* Remove from heat; stir in coffee liqueur.

2. Pour eggnog into individual mugs. Top with whipped cream, if desired.

MAKES 8 SERVINGS

Pumpkin Custard

Fruit Mousse

1 cup whipping cream
1 teaspoon vanilla
1 package (3 ounces) cream cheese, softened
½ cup strawberry or seedless raspberry fruit spread
Fresh berries

1. Beat cream and vanilla in medium bowl with electric mixer at high speed until stiff peaks form. Transfer to small bowl. Beat cream cheese in same medium bowl at medium speed until creamy. Blend in fruit spread. Fold in whipped cream.

2. Spoon into individual dessert dishes; chill at least 2 hours or up to 24 hours before serving. Serve with fresh berries.

MAKES 6 SERVINGS

Mandarin Orange Mold

1¾ cups boiling water
2 packages (4-serving size each) orange flavor gelatin
3 cups ice cubes
1 can (15.25 ounces) DOLE® Tropical Fruit, drained
1 can (11 ounces) DOLE® Mandarin Oranges, drained

• Stir boiling water into gelatin in large bowl at least 2 minutes until completely dissolved. Add ice cubes. Stir until ice is melted and gelatin is thickened. Stir in tropical fruit and mandarin oranges. Spoon into 6-cup mold.

• Refrigerate 4 hours or until firm. Unmold.* Garnish as desired.

*To unmold, dip mold in warm water about 15 seconds. Gently pull gelatin from around edges with moist fingers. Place moistened serving plate on top of mold. Invert mold and plate. Holding mold and plate together, shake slightly to loosen. Gently remove mold.

MAKES 12 SERVINGS

Fruit Mousse

Pear and Raspberry Strudel

½ cup raspberry fruit spread
½ teaspoon ground cinnamon
4 medium ripe pears, peeled, cored and thinly sliced
1½ cups fresh raspberries
10 sheets phyllo dough (about 18×14 inches)
Butter-flavored nonstick cooking spray
Ice cream (optional)

1. Preheat oven to 350°F. Combine fruit spread and cinnamon in small bowl; set aside. Combine pears and raspberries in large bowl.

2. Place 1 sheet phyllo dough on work surface. Keep remaining sheets covered with plastic wrap and damp kitchen towel. Lightly coat first phyllo sheet with cooking spray. Place second sheet on top of first; spray with cooking spray. Repeat process with remaining phyllo sheets.

3. Add fruit spread mixture to fruit. Spread fruit filling on phyllo to within 2 inches of edges. Starting at short sides, fold each over filling once. Beginning at long side, roll up jelly-roll fashion for roll about 14×5 inches. Place in jelly-roll pan. Lightly coat strudel with cooking spray. Cut diagonal slits about 1 inch apart and ½ inch deep along top of strudel.

4. Bake 30 minutes or until lightly browned. Cool 30 minutes. Slice diagonally into 12 pieces. Serve warm with ice cream, if desired.

MAKES 12 SERVINGS

Oregon Hot Apple Cider

8 cups apple cider
½ cup dried cherries
½ cup dried cranberries
3 cinnamon sticks, broken in half
8 whole cloves
1 pear, quartered, cored and sliced

Combine cider, cherries, cranberries, cinnamon sticks and cloves in large saucepan. Heat just to a simmer. *Do not boil.* Add pear just before serving.

MAKES 16 (½-CUP) SERVINGS

Pear and Raspberry Strudel

Chocolate Cookie Parfaits

1 package (4-serving size) chocolate instant pudding and pie filling mix
2 cups milk
8 tablespoons thawed whipped topping
4 chocolate sandwich cookies, finely crushed
4 teaspoons multi-colored sprinkles

1. Prepare pudding according to package directions using 2 cups milk.

2. Spoon half of pudding in four parfait glasses or clear plastic cups. Spread 1 tablespoon whipped topping over pudding in each glass. Sprinkle with half of crushed cookies. Layer remaining pudding over top of cookies. Top with remaining whipped topping, cookies and sprinkles.

MAKES 4 SERVINGS

Cinnamon-Raisin-Apple Bread Pudding

1 large Granny Smith apple, peeled and cut into ½-inch pieces
¾ cup plus 2 tablespoons sugar, divided
1 teaspoon cinnamon
3½ cups diced cinnamon-raisin bread (about 8 slices)
3 eggs
2 cups milk
¼ cup (½ stick) butter, melted and cooled
¼ teaspoon salt
Prepared caramel or butterscotch sauce, warmed

1. Preheat oven to 350°F. Grease 1½-quart baking dish; set aside. Combine apple, 2 tablespoons sugar and cinnamon in large bowl; mix well. Add bread cubes; toss to combine. Transfer mixture to prepared dish.

2. Beat eggs lightly in medium bowl. Add remaining ¾ cup sugar; beat well. Stir in milk, butter and salt; mix well. Pour over bread mixture. Press down so that bread is coated with milk mixture. Let stand 10 minutes (or cover and refrigerate overnight).

3. Bake 50 minutes or until puffed and golden brown. Cool on wire rack at least 20 minutes. Serve with caramel sauce.

MAKES 6 TO 8 SERVINGS

Chocolate Cookie Parfaits

Raspberry Mousse

1 package (10 ounces) frozen raspberries in syrup
1 package (4-serving size) raspberry-flavored gelatin
¼ cup water
2 cups whipping cream

1. Process raspberries with syrup in food processor or blender until smooth. Press through fine mesh sieve to remove seeds. Set aside.

2. Heat gelatin and water in small saucepan over medium heat 5 to 7 minutes or until mixture is very syrupy, stirring occasionally. Remove from heat. Cool slightly.

3. Beat cream in large bowl with electric mixer at high speed 3 to 5 minutes or until soft peaks form. Add raspberries and gelatin mixture; beat 3 to 5 minutes or until well blended.

4. Pour into individual serving dishes; refrigerate 2 hours or until set.

MAKES 4 CUPS

Spiced Pears with Vanilla Ice Cream

1 sheet (18×12 inches) heavy-duty foil
2 teaspoons butter, softened
1 tablespoon light brown sugar
¼ teaspoon pumpkin pie spice
1 large Bosc pear, halved lengthwise and cored
  Lemon juice
2 scoops vanilla ice cream

1. Preheat oven to 450°F. Coat center of foil with butter.

2. Combine brown sugar and pumpkin pie spice in small bowl; stir to blend. Sprinkle sugar mixture over butter. Sprinkle cut sides of pear halves with lemon juice. Place pear halves, cut side down, side by side on sugar mixture.

3. Double fold sides and ends of foil to seal foil packet, leaving headspace for heat circulation. Place packet on small baking sheet.

4. Bake 40 minutes or until pear halves are tender. Remove from oven. Let stand 15 minutes.

5. Open packet and transfer pear halves to serving plates. Spoon sauce over pears. Serve with ice cream.

MAKES 2 SERVINGS

Raspberry Mousse

Cranberry Crunch Gelatin

2 cups boiling water

2 packages (4-serving size each) cherry-flavored gelatin

1 can (16 ounces) whole berry cranberry sauce

1½ cups mini marshmallows

1 cup coarsely chopped walnuts

1. Stir boiling water into gelatin in large bowl 2 minutes or until completely dissolved. Chill about 2 hours or until slightly set.

2. Fold cranberry sauce, marshmallows and walnuts into gelatin mixture. Pour into 6-cup gelatin mold. Cover; refrigerate at least 4 hours or until set. Remove from mold.

MAKES 8 SERVINGS

Easy Cocoa Mix

2 cups nonfat dry milk powder

1 cup sugar

¾ cup powdered nondairy creamer

½ cup unsweetened cocoa powder

¼ teaspoon salt

¾ cup boiling water

Sweetened whipped cream (optional)

Marshmallows (optional)

Combine milk powder, sugar, creamer, cocoa and salt in medium bowl; stir until well blended. Place rounded ¼ cup cocoa mix in mug or cup; add ¾ cup boiling water. Stir until mix is dissolved. Top with sweetened whipped cream and marshmallows, if desired. Serve immediately. Spoon any remaining cocoa mix into large resealable food storage bag.

MAKES ABOUT 4 CUPS MIX OR 16 SERVINGS

Cocoa Marshmallow Mix: Prepare Easy Cocoa Mix; add 1 package (10½ ounces) miniature marshmallows. Place rounded ½ cup cocoa mix in mug or cup. Follow recipe as directed above.

Cranberry Crunch Gelatin

White Chocolate Bavarian Christmas Tree

Ingredients

- 1 cup half-and-half
- 2 teaspoons vanilla
- 2 envelopes unflavored gelatin
- 6 eggs, separated
- 12 ounces white or semisweet chocolate
- 1 teaspoon cream of tartar
- 1½ cups whipping cream, whipped

Decorations: Candy spearmint leaves, red cinnamon candies, red candy-coated licorice pieces, green mini jaw breakers

Supplies

8-cup tree mold or other decorative mold

1. Combine half-and-half and vanilla in medium saucepan. Sprinkle gelatin over mixture; let stand 5 minutes. Stir over low heat until gelatin is completely dissolved.

2. Beat egg yolks in small bowl with electric mixer on low speed until blended. Stir about ½ cup gelatin mixture into egg yolks; return egg yolk mixture to saucepan. Cook and stir over low heat until thick enough to coat the back of a spoon.

3. Melt chocolate in top of double boiler over hot, not boiling, water, stirring constantly. Stir gelatin mixture into chocolate. Remove from heat; cool to room temperature.

4. Beat egg whites and cream of tartar in large bowl until stiff peaks form. Gently fold cooled chocolate mixture into beaten egg whites. Fold in whipped cream.

5. Spoon mixture into 8-cup tree mold. Refrigerate 8 hours or until set.

6. To unmold, pull chocolate mixture from edge of mold with moistened fingers. Or, run small metal spatula or pointed knife dipped in warm water around edge of mold. Dip bottom of mold briefly in warm water. Place serving plate on top of mold. Invert mold and plate; shake to loosen chocolate mixture. Gently remove mold. Decorate with candies as desired.

MAKES 12 TO 14 SERVINGS

Gingered Pumpkin Custard

¾ cup sugar

2 eggs

1½ teaspoons ground cinnamon

½ teaspoon salt

½ teaspoon ground nutmeg

1 can (15 ounces) solid-pack pumpkin

1¼ cups half-and-half

3 tablespoons chopped candied ginger

Sweetened whipped cream

Candy sprinkles

1. Preheat oven to 375°F. Grease 8-inch glass baking dish or 1½-quart casserole with nonstick cooking spray.

2. Combine sugar, eggs, cinnamon, salt and nutmeg in medium bowl; mix well. Add pumpkin and half-and-half; mix until well blended. Pour into prepared dish. Sprinkle ginger evenly over top of pumpkin mixture.

3. Bake 45 minutes or until knife inserted into center comes out clean. Cool on wire rack 20 minutes before serving. Serve with whipped cream and sprinkles, if desired.

MAKES 6 TO 8 SERVINGS

Variation: For individual servings, pour custard mixture into six or eight ramekins or custard cups. Place on baking sheet. Bake 35 to 40 minutes or until knife inserted into centers comes out clean.

Caramel Candy Bar Pudding

⅔ cup sugar

3 tablespoons cocoa powder

2 tablespoons ARGO® Corn Starch

¼ teaspoon salt

2 cups milk

2 egg yolks

2 tablespoons butter

1 teaspoon SPICE ISLANDS® Pure Vanilla Extract

½ cup caramel ice cream topping

6 tablespoons chopped peanuts

Whipped topping (optional)

MIX sugar, cocoa, corn starch and salt in a large microwave-safe bowl. Whisk in milk and egg yolks until well blended.

MICROWAVE on HIGH (100%) power for 5 to 7 minutes, stirring every 1 to 2 minutes. Cook until pudding is thick and has boiled at least 1 minute. Remove from microwave. Stir in butter and vanilla. Cover surface with plastic wrap.

CHILL 2 hours.

SPOON pudding into individual clear bowls or stemware. Top with caramel topping and peanuts. Garnish with whipped topping, if desired.

MAKES 6 SERVINGS

Hot Buttered Cider

⅓ cup packed brown sugar

¼ cup (½ stick) butter, softened

¼ cup honey

¼ teaspoon ground cinnamon

¼ teaspoon ground nutmeg

Apple cider or juice

1. Beat brown sugar, butter, honey, cinnamon and nutmeg with electric mixer at high speed until well blended and fluffy. Place butter mixture in tightly covered container. Refrigerate up to two weeks. Bring butter mixture to room temperature before using.

2. To serve, heat apple cider in large saucepan over medium heat until hot. Fill individual mugs with hot apple cider; stir in 1 tablespoon butter mixture per 1 cup apple cider.

MAKES 12 SERVINGS

Caramel Candy Bar Pudding

Raspberry-Orange Trifle
with White Chocolate Custard

1   package (16 ounces) pound cake mix, plus ingredients to prepare mix

1½ teaspoons orange extract

1   package (4-serving size) white chocolate instant pudding and pie filling mix

1   cup cold milk

2   tablespoons dry sherry

1   cup red raspberry preserves or jam

    Red raspberries, kiwi slices* or peach slices

    Whipped cream

    Slivered almonds, toasted**

Cut an unpeeled kiwi into slices, then cut out rounds from the flesh using a small biscuit or cookie cutter, leaving the peel behind. Use a fluted cutter for a more decorative look.

**To toast almonds, spread in single layer on baking sheet. Bake in preheated 350°F oven 5 to 7 minutes or until lightly toasted, stirring occasionally.*

1. Preheat oven to 350°F. Spray 9×5-inch loaf pan with nonstick cooking spray.

2. Prepare pound cake mix according to package directions; stir in orange extract. Spread batter in prepared pan; bake according to package directions. Cool in pan 15 minutes; remove to wire rack to cool completely.

3. Combine pudding mix and milk in medium bowl; whisk until smooth. Cover and refrigerate 30 minutes.

4. Trim off browned bottom, edges and top of cake; discard. Cut cake into 1-inch cubes. Place cake cubes in large bowl; sprinkle with sherry. Place raspberry preserves in small microwavable bowl; microwave on HIGH 5 to 10 seconds or just until preserves begin to melt.

5. Layer cake cubes, raspberry preserves, pudding and fruit in dessert dishes or martini glasses. Top with whipped cream; sprinkle with almonds.

MAKES 8 TO 10 SERVINGS

Serving Suggestion: Layer all ingredients—cake cubes, sauce, pudding and fruit in large glass serving bowl. Trifle may be served immediately; however, flavors will develop and be more pronounced if dessert is prepared at least 2 hours before serving.

Raspberry-Orange Trifle
with White Chocolate Custard

Almond-Pear Strudel

    5   to 6 cups thinly sliced crisp pears (4 to 5 medium pears)
    1   tablespoon grated lemon peel
    1   tablespoon lemon juice
    ⅓   cup plus 1 teaspoon sugar, divided
    2   teaspoons ground cinnamon
    1   teaspoon ground nutmeg
    6   sheets (¼ pound) phyllo dough
    ¼   cup (½ stick) butter, melted
    ½   teaspoon almond extract
    ¾   cup slivered almonds, toasted* and divided

To toast almonds, spread in single layer on baking sheet. Bake in preheated 350°F oven 5 to 7 minutes or until lightly toasted, stirring occasionally.

1. Preheat oven to 300°F.

2. Place sliced pears in large microwavable bowl. Stir in lemon peel and lemon juice. Microwave on HIGH 6 minutes or until tender; cool. Combine ⅓ cup sugar, cinnamon and nutmeg in small bowl; set aside.

3. Cover work surface with plastic wrap. Place 1 phyllo sheet in middle of plastic wrap. (Cover remaining phyllo dough with damp kitchen towel to prevent dough from drying out.) Brush 1 teaspoon melted butter onto phyllo sheet. Place second phyllo sheet over first; brush with 1 teaspoon butter. Repeat layering with remaining sheets of phyllo.

4. *Increase oven temperature to 400°F.* Spray baking sheet with nonstick cooking spray. Drain pears and toss with sugar mixture and almond extract.

5. Spread pear mixture evenly over phyllo, leaving 3-inch strip on far long side. Sprinkle pears with ½ cup almonds. Brush strip with 2 teaspoons butter. Beginning at long side of phyllo closest to you, carefully roll up jelly-roll style, using plastic wrap to gently lift, forming strudel. Place strudel, seam side down, on prepared baking sheet. Brush top with 1 teaspoon butter.

6. Bake 20 minutes or until golden. Brush with remaining butter. Sprinkle with remaining ¼ cup almonds and 1 teaspoon sugar. Bake 5 minutes. Cool 10 minutes before serving.

MAKES 8 SERVINGS

Almond-Pear Strudel

French Yule Log

Powdered sugar

4 eggs, separated

¾ cup sugar, divided

¾ cup ground blanched almonds

⅓ cup all-purpose flour

⅓ cup HERSHEY'S® Cocoa

½ teaspoon baking soda

¼ teaspoon salt

¼ cup water

1 teaspoon vanilla extract

¼ teaspoon almond extract

Whipped Cream Filling (page 259)

Creamy Cocoa Frosting (page 259)

1. Heat oven to 375°F. Line 15½×10½×1-inch jelly-roll pan with foil; generously grease foil. Sift powdered sugar onto clean towel.

2. Beat egg yolks in medium bowl 3 minutes on medium speed of mixer. Gradually add ½ cup sugar, beating another 2 minutes until thick and lemon-colored. Combine almonds, flour, cocoa, baking soda and salt; add alternately with water to egg yolk mixture, beating on low speed just until blended. Stir in vanilla and almond extracts.

3. Beat egg whites in large bowl until foamy. Gradually add ¼ cup sugar, beating until stiff peaks form. Carefully fold chocolate mixture into beaten egg whites. Spread batter evenly in prepared pan.

4. Bake 16 to 18 minutes or until top springs back when lightly touched. Cool in pan on wire rack 10 minutes; remove from pan onto prepared towel. Carefully remove foil. Cool completely.

5. Cut into four equal rectangles approximately 3½×10 inches. Chill layers while preparing filling and frosting. Place one cake layer on serving plate. Spread one-third (about 1 cup) Whipped Cream Filling evenly over cake layer; top with another cake layer. Repeat with remaining cake and filling, ending with cake layer. Refrigerate about 1 hour before frosting. Generously frost loaf with Creamy Cocoa Frosting. Swirl frosting with spatula or score with fork to resemble bark. Refrigerate at least 4 hours before serving. Garnish with shaved chocolate and chocolate leaves, if desired. Cover; refrigerate leftover dessert.

MAKES 10 TO 12 SERVINGS

Whipped Cream Filling

1½ cups cold whipping cream

⅓ cup powdered sugar

1 teaspoon vanilla extract

Combine whipping cream, powdered sugar and vanilla in large bowl. Beat until cream is stiff. (Do not overbeat.)

MAKES ABOUT 3 CUPS

Creamy Cocoa Frosting

3½ cups powdered sugar

½ cup HERSHEY'S® Cocoa

½ cup (1 stick) butter or margarine, softened

2 tablespoons light corn syrup

2 teaspoons vanilla extract

⅓ cup milk

Combine powdered sugar and cocoa. Beat butter, ½ cup cocoa mixture, corn syrup and vanilla in medium bowl until smooth. Add remaining cocoa mixture alternately with milk, beating until smooth and of spreading consistency.

MAKES 2½ CUPS

Mocha Coffee

⅔ cup unsweetened cocoa powder

½ cup nonfat dry milk

½ cup powdered sugar

⅓ cup granulated sugar

¼ cup instant coffee granules

1½ teaspoons ground cinnamon

½ teaspoon ground nutmeg

16 cups hot milk

Combine cocoa, dry milk, powdered sugar, granulated sugar, coffee granules, cinnamon and nutmeg in large bowl; stir to blend. Spoon 2 tablespoons cocoa mixture into each cup or mug. Stir 1 cup hot milk into each cup. Serve warm.

MAKES 16 SERVINGS

Single-Serving Variation: Follow recipe as instructed, but store the remaining cocoa mixture in large resealable container for later use.

Mocha Coffee

Pumpkin-Cranberry Custard

1 can (30 ounces) pumpkin pie filling
1 can (12 ounces) evaporated milk
1 cup dried cranberries
4 eggs, beaten
1 cup whole gingersnap cookies (optional)
   Whipped cream (optional)

Slow Cooker Directions

Combine pumpkin, evaporated milk, cranberries and eggs in slow cooker; mix thoroughly. Cover; cook on HIGH 4 to 4½ hours. Serve with gingersnaps and whipped cream, if desired.

MAKE 4 TO 6 SERVINGS

Baked Pear Dessert

⅓ cup unsweetened apple cider or apple juice, divided
2 tablespoons dried cranberries or raisins
1 tablespoon toasted sliced almonds*
⅛ teaspoon ground cinnamon
1 medium unpeeled pear (about 6 ounces), cut in half lengthwise and cored
½ cup vanilla ice cream or frozen yogurt

To toast almonds, spread in single layer on baking sheet. Bake in preheated 350°F oven 5 to 7 minutes or until lightly toasted, stirring occasionally.

1. Preheat oven to 350°F. Combine 1 tablespoon cider, cranberries, almonds and cinnamon in small bowl.

2. Place pear halves, cut sides up, in small baking dish. Evenly mound almond mixture on top of pear halves. Pour remaining cider into dish; cover with foil.

3. Bake 35 to 40 minutes or until pears are soft, spooning cider in dish over pears once or twice during baking. Serve warm with ice cream.

MAKES 2 SERVINGS

Pumpkin-Cranberry Custard

Chocolate Hazelnut Mousse

1 package (4-serving size) chocolate instant pudding and pie filling mix

2 cups milk

½ cup chocolate hazelnut spread

1½ cups light whipped topping, plus additional for garnish (optional)

Fresh strawberries, halved (optional)

1. Prepare pudding with milk according to package directions. Whisk in hazelnut spread. Refrigerate 15 minutes.

2. Fold 1½ cups whipped topping into pudding. Spoon mixture into small bowls or ramekins. Refrigerate until ready to serve. Garnish with dollop of whipped topping and strawberries.

MAKES 8 SERVINGS

Cranberry-Apple Strudel

Butter-flavored nonstick cooking spray

1 tablespoon butter

1 tablespoon packed light brown sugar

2 medium Golden Delicious apples, cored, peeled and diced

¼ cup raisins

1 can (16 ounces) whole-berry cranberry sauce

6 sheets phyllo dough

3 tablespoons graham cracker crumbs, divided

¼ cup toasted* almonds, chopped

*To toast almonds, spread in single layer on baking sheet. Bake in preheated 350°F oven 5 to 7 minutes or until lightly toasted, stirring occasionally.

1. Preheat oven to 375°F. Spray cookie sheet with cooking spray. Melt butter in large saucepan over medium heat. Add brown sugar; bring to a boil. Add apples and raisins; cook 10 minutes or until apples are tender. Remove from heat. Add cranberry sauce; mix well. Set aside.

2. Place 1 sheet of phyllo on piece of parchment paper with narrow side farthest away. Spray phyllo with cooking spray; sprinkle 1½ teaspoons graham cracker crumbs on phyllo. Overlap second sheet of phyllo over first sheet about 1 inch down from top. Spray with cooking spray; sprinkle with 1½ teaspoons crumbs. Continue overlapping with remaining phyllo and crumbs, spraying with cooking spray between each layer.

3. Spoon cooled cranberry mixture into center of phyllo. Sprinkle chopped almonds over mixture. Fold bottom and sides of phyllo to cover mixture, forming an envelope. With floured hands, roll filled phyllo, jelly-roll fashion, to form strudel. Place strudel on prepared cookie sheet. Spray top with cooking spray. Make eight diagonal cuts across top of strudel. Bake 12 to 15 minutes or until lightly browned. Cool on wire rack 30 minutes. Cut crosswise into eight pieces.

MAKES 8 SERVINGS

Chocolate Hazelnut Mousse

FESTIVE
CAKES, PIES & TARTS

Celebration Pumpkin Cake

- 1 package (about 18 ounces) spice cake mix
- 1 can (15 ounces) solid-pack pumpkin
- 3 eggs
- ¼ cup (½ stick) butter, softened
- 1½ containers (16 ounces each) cream cheese frosting
- ⅓ cup caramel ice cream topping
  Pecan halves (optional)

1. Preheat oven to 350°F. Grease and flour three 9-inch round cake pans.

2. Beat cake mix, pumpkin, eggs and butter in large bowl with electric mixer at medium speed until blended. Pour batter into prepared pans.

3. Bake 20 minutes or until toothpick inserted into centers comes out clean. Cool in pans 15 minutes. Remove to wire racks; cool completely.

4. Place one cake layer on serving plate; spread with one fourth of frosting. Repeat layers. Top with remaining cake layer. Frost cake with remaining frosting. Spread caramel topping over top of cake, allowing some to drip down side. Garnish with pecans.

MAKES 12 SERVINGS

Tip: This cake is perfect for preparing a day or two ahead of your get-together because the pumpkin added to the cake mix helps it stay nice and moist.

Celebration Pumpkin Cake

Spiced Raisin Custard Pie

1½ cups raisins

1 teaspoon sugar

1 teaspoon ground cinnamon

1 can (14 ounces) sweetened condensed milk

1 cup biscuit and baking mix

1 cup applesauce

½ cup sugar

3 eggs

¼ cup (½ stick) butter, melted

2 teaspoons ground cinnamon

2 teaspoons vanilla

1 teaspoon ground nutmeg

1 container (8 ounces) frozen nondairy whipped topping, thawed

1. Preheat oven to 325°F. Spray 10-inch glass pie plate with nonstick cooking spray.

2. Place raisins in small bowl, separating any that may be stuck together. Combine sugar and cinnamon in small bowl. Reserve 1 teaspoon cinnamon-sugar mixture. Sprinkle half over raisins; set remaining aside. Toss to coat.

3. Combine condensed milk, baking mix, applesauce, sugar, eggs, butter, cinnamon, vanilla and nutmeg in large bowl; beat 2 minutes with electric mixer on medium speed until well blended. Pour into prepared pie plate. Bake 10 minutes.

4. Remove from oven; top with spiced raisins and sprinkle with reserved cinnamon-sugar mixture. Bake 35 to 40 minutes (center will be soft). Cool to room temperature; refrigerate at least 2 hours. Serve chilled with whipped topping. Refrigerate any leftover pie.

MAKES 12 SERVINGS

Spiced Raisin Custard Pie

White Chocolate Cranberry Tart

1 refrigerated pie crust

1 cup sugar

2 eggs

¼ cup (½ stick) butter, melted

2 teaspoons vanilla

½ cup all-purpose flour

6 squares (1 ounce each) white chocolate, chopped

½ cup chopped macadamia nuts, lightly toasted*

½ cup dried cranberries, coarsely chopped

*Toast chopped macadamia nuts in small skillet over medium heat about 3 minutes or until fragrant.

1. Preheat oven to 350°F. Place pie crust in 9-inch tart pan with removable bottom or pie pan. (Refrigerate or freeze other crust for another use.)

2. Combine sugar, eggs, butter and vanilla in large bowl; mix well. Stir in flour until well blended. Add white chocolate, macadamia nuts and cranberries.

3. Pour filling into unbaked crust. Bake 50 to 55 minutes or until top of tart is crusty and deep golden brown, and knife inserted into center comes out clean. Cool completely on wire rack.

MAKES 8 SERVINGS

Serve it with Style!: Top each serving with a dollop of whipped cream flavored with ground cinnamon, a favorite liqueur and/or grated orange peel, fresh cranberries and white chocolate shavings.

White Chocolate Cranberry Tart

Fall Harvest Spice Cake

1 package (about 18 ounces) spice or carrot cake mix
1 cup water
3 eggs
⅓ cup vegetable oil
⅓ cup apple butter
   Maple Buttercream Frosting (recipe follows)
2 cups coarsely chopped walnuts

1. Preheat oven to 375°F. Grease and flour two 9-inch round cake pans.

2. Combine cake mix, water, eggs, oil and apple butter in medium bowl. Beat with electric mixer at low speed until blended; beat at medium speed 2 minutes. Pour batter into prepared pans.

3. Bake 35 to 40 minutes or until toothpick inserted into centers comes out clean. Cool in pans on wire racks 10 minutes. Remove to racks; cool completely.

4. Prepare Maple Buttercream Frosting.

5. Place 1 cake layer on serving plate; frost top with Maple Buttercream Frosting. Top with second cake layer; frost top and side. Press walnuts onto side of cake.

MAKES 12 SERVINGS

Maple Buttercream Frosting

½ cup (1 stick) butter, softened
½ cup maple or pancake syrup
3 cups powdered sugar

Beat butter and syrup in medium bowl with electric mixer at low speed until blended. Gradually beat in powdered sugar until smooth.

MAKES ABOUT 2 CUPS

Fall Harvest Spice Cake

Country Pecan Pie

Pie pastry for single 9-inch pie crust

1¼ cups dark corn syrup

4 eggs

½ cup packed light brown sugar

¼ cup (½ stick) butter, melted

2 teaspoons all-purpose flour

1½ teaspoons vanilla

1½ cups pecan halves

1. Preheat oven to 350°F. Roll pastry on lightly floured surface to form 13-inch circle. Fit into 9-inch pie plate. Trim edges; flute. Set aside.

2. Beat corn syrup, eggs, brown sugar and butter in large bowl with electric mixer at medium speed 2 to 3 minutes or until well blended. Stir in flour and vanilla until blended. Pour into unbaked pie crust. Arrange pecans on top.

3. Bake 40 to 45 minutes or until center of filling is puffed and golden brown. Cool completely on wire rack.

MAKES 8 SERVINGS

Nutty Cheesecake Bites

1 (8-ounce) package cream cheese, softened

½ cup SKIPPY® Creamy Peanut Butter

¼ cup sugar

¼ teaspoon ground cinnamon

¼ teaspoon vanilla extract

Finely chopped peanuts or unsweetened shredded coconut

1. In medium bowl, combine all ingredients except peanuts. Beat with electric mixer on medium speed, scraping down side of bowl as needed. Refrigerate 30 minutes or until firm.

2. Roll dough into ¾-inch balls; roll balls in peanuts. Refrigerate 15 minutes before serving.

MAKES 30 BITES

Tip: Also terrific with SKIPPY® Natural Creamy Peanut Butter Spread.

Country Pecan Pie

Walnut Tartlets
with Chocolate Ganache Filling

Chocolate Leaves (page 277)
½ cup walnut halves, toasted*
1 cup all-purpose flour
¼ cup sugar
1 tablespoon grated lemon peel
⅓ cup butter, cut into pieces
1 egg, lightly beaten
Chocolate Ganache (page 277)

To toast walnuts, spread in single layer on baking sheet. Bake in preheated 350°F oven 8 to 10 minutes or until lightly browned, stirring frequently.

1. Prepare Chocolate Leaves. Set aside.

2. Preheat oven to 350°F. Place walnuts in food processor. Process using on/off pulsing action until walnuts are finely chopped, but not pasty.

3. Reserve 2 tablespoons walnuts. Place remaining walnuts in medium bowl. Add flour, sugar and lemon peel; blend well. Cut in butter with pastry blender or two knives until mixture resembles coarse crumbs. Stir in egg with fork until mixture holds together.

4. Spoon 2 teaspoonfuls mixture into ungreased mini-muffin cups. Press dough onto bottom and up side of each cup with fingers.

5. Bake 16 to 20 minutes or until golden brown. Cool 5 minutes in pan. Remove shells from pans. Cool completely on wire racks.

6. Prepare Chocolate Ganache. Spoon ½ teaspoon ganache into each shell. Sprinkle reserved 2 tablespoons chopped nuts evenly over shells. Gently push Chocolate Leaf into each shell.

7. Store tightly covered in refrigerator up to one week.

MAKES 30 TARTLETS

Chocolate Ganache

2 tablespoons whipping cream
1 tablespoon butter
½ cup (2 ounces) chopped semisweet chocolate or semisweet chocolate chips
½ teaspoon vanilla

Heat whipping cream and butter in small saucepan over medium heat until butter melts and mixture boils, stirring frequently with wooden spoon. Remove saucepan from heat. Stir in chocolate and vanilla until mixture is smooth, returning to heat for 20 to 30 second intervals as needed to melt chocolate. Keep warm (ganache is semi-firm at room temperature).

MAKES ABOUT ⅓ CUP

Chocolate Leaves

½ cup (2 ounces) chopped semisweet chocolate or semisweet chocolate chips
1 teaspoon shortening
   Assorted nontoxic fresh leaves such as rose, lemon or camellia,* cleaned and dried

Nontoxic leaves are available in florist shops.

1. Place large sheet heavy-duty foil on counter.

2. Fill saucepan one-fourth full (about 1 inch deep) with warm water. Place chocolate and shortening in 1-cup glass measure. To melt chocolate, place measure in warm water; stir frequently with rubber spatula until smooth. (Be careful not to get any water into chocolate or chocolate may become lumpy.)

3. Brush melted chocolate onto underside of each leaf with small, clean craft paintbrush or pastry brush, coating leaf thickly and evenly. Carefully wipe off any chocolate that may have run onto front of leaf.

4. Place leaves, chocolate-sides up, on foil. Let stand 1 hour or until chocolate is set.

5. Carefully peel leaves away from chocolate beginning at stem ends; refrigerate Chocolate Leaves until ready to use.

MAKES 30 TO 40 LEAVES

Traditional Fruit Cake

- 3 cups walnut halves
- 1 package (8 ounces) candied cherries
- 1 package (8 ounces) chopped dates
- 1 package (4 ounces) candied pineapple
- ¾ cup all-purpose flour
- ¾ cup sugar
- ½ teaspoon baking powder
- ½ teaspoon salt
- 3 eggs, lightly beaten
- 3 tablespoons dark rum or rum extract
- 1 tablespoon grated orange peel
- 1 teaspoon vanilla

1. Preheat oven to 300°F. Line 9×5-inch loaf pan with parchment paper; spray with nonstick cooking spray.

2. Combine walnuts and fruit in large bowl. Combine flour, sugar, baking powder and salt in medium bowl. Sift into walnut mixture; toss gently to coat. Stir in eggs, rum, orange peel and vanilla. Spread batter in prepared pan.

3. Bake 1 hour 45 minutes or until golden brown. Cool completely in pan on wire rack.

MAKES 1 LOAF

Traditional Fruit Cake

LIBBY'S® Famous Pumpkin Pie

¾ cup granulated sugar

1 teaspoon ground cinnamon

½ teaspoon salt

½ teaspoon ground ginger

¼ teaspoon ground cloves

2 large eggs

1 can (15 ounces) LIBBY'S® 100% Pure Pumpkin

1 can (12 fluid ounces) NESTLÉ® CARNATION® Evaporated Milk

1 *unbaked* 9-inch (4-cup volume) deep-dish pie shell

Whipped cream

MIX sugar, cinnamon, salt, ginger and cloves in small bowl. Beat eggs in large bowl. Stir in pumpkin and sugar-spice mixture. Gradually stir in evaporated milk.

POUR into pie shell.

BAKE in preheated 425°F oven for 15 minutes. Reduce oven temperature to 350°F; bake for 40 to 50 minutes or until knife inserted near center comes out clean. Cool on wire rack for 2 hours. Serve immediately or refrigerate. Top with whipped cream before serving.

MAKES 8 SERVINGS

Note: Do not freeze this pie because this will result in the crust separating from the filling.

Tip: You can substitute *1¾ teaspoons* pumpkin pie spice for the cinnamon, ginger and cloves; however, the flavor will be slightly different.

For 2 shallow pies: Substitute two 9-inch (2-cup volume) pie shells. Bake in preheated 425°F oven for 15 minutes. Reduce temperature to 350°F; bake for 20 to 30 minutes or until pies test done.

LIBBY'S® Famous Pumpkin Pie

Oats 'n' Apple Tart

1½ cups quick oats

½ cup packed brown sugar, divided

1 tablespoon plus ¼ teaspoon ground cinnamon, divided

5 tablespoons butter, melted

2 medium sweet apples, such as Golden Delicious, unpeeled, cored and thinly sliced

1 teaspoon lemon juice

¼ cup water

1 envelope (¼ ounce) unflavored gelatin

½ cup apple juice concentrate

1 package (8 ounces) cream cheese, softened

⅛ teaspoon ground nutmeg

Sprigs fresh mint (optional)

1. Preheat oven to 350°F. Combine oats, ¼ cup brown sugar and 1 tablespoon cinnamon in medium bowl. Add butter and stir until combined. Press onto bottom and up side of 9-inch pie plate. Bake 7 minutes or until set. Cool on wire rack.

2. Toss apple slices with lemon juice in small bowl; set aside. Place water in small saucepan. Sprinkle gelatin over water; let stand 3 to 5 minutes. Stir in apple juice concentrate; cook and stir over medium heat until gelatin is dissolved. *Do not boil.* Remove from heat and set aside.

3. Beat cream cheese in medium bowl with electric mixer at medium speed until fluffy and smooth. Add remaining ¼ cup brown sugar, ¼ teaspoon cinnamon and nutmeg; mix until smooth. Slowly beat in gelatin mixture on low speed 1 minute or until blended and creamy. *Do not overbeat.*

4. Arrange apple slices in crust. Pour cream cheese mixture evenly over top. Refrigerate 2 hours or until set. Garnish with mint.

MAKES 8 SERVINGS

Oats 'n' Apple Tart

Ginger-Crusted Pumpkin Cheesecake

12 whole honey graham crackers, broken into small pieces

3 tablespoons butter, melted

½ teaspoon ground ginger

1 can (15 ounces) solid-pack pumpkin

3 packages (8 ounces each) cream cheese, softened

1 cup sugar

4 eggs

½ cup evaporated milk

1 tablespoon vanilla

1 teaspoon ground cinnamon

½ teaspoon ground nutmeg, plus additional for topping

¼ teaspoon salt

2 cups frozen whipped topping, thawed

1. Preheat oven to 350°F. Spray 9-inch springform pan with nonstick cooking spray.

2. Place graham crackers, butter and ginger in food processor or blender; process using on/off pulsing action until coarse crumbs are formed. Gently press crumb mixture onto bottom and ¾ inch up side of pan. Bake 10 minutes or until lightly browned. Cool slightly in pan on wire rack.

3. Beat pumpkin, cream cheese, sugar, eggs, evaporated milk, vanilla, cinnamon, ½ teaspoon nutmeg and salt in large bowl with electric mixer at medium-high speed until smooth; pour into crust.

4. Bake 1 hour and 15 minutes or until top begins to crack and center is almost set. Cool in pan on wire rack 1 hour. Cover; refrigerate until ready to serve.

5. Top each slice with whipped topping and sprinkle with additional nutmeg, just before serving.

MAKES 16 SERVINGS

Cook's Tip: This cheesecake freezes well. In fact, the flavors improve with freezing!

Ginger-Crusted Pumpkin Cheesecake

Peanut Butter Cream Pie

½ cup SKIPPY® Creamy Peanut Butter

⅓ cup sugar

1 (8-ounce) package cream cheese, softened

1 (8-ounce) container frozen whipped topping, thawed and divided

1 (9-inch) chocolate crumb crust

1 cup hot fudge topping, at room temperature

Melted SKIPPY® Peanut Butter, if desired

1. In large bowl, beat together peanut butter, sugar and cream cheese with electric mixer on medium speed, scraping down side of bowl occasionally, 2 minutes or until smooth. Fold in half of whipped topping.

2. Evenly spoon peanut butter mixture into crust, then evenly spread fudge topping over peanut butter mixture; top with remaining half of whipped topping. Refrigerate at least 3 hours before serving. Drizzle with additional melted peanut butter.

MAKES 8 SERVINGS

Tip: Peanut Butter Cream Pie can be frozen. Thaw 30 minutes before serving.

Hazelnut Plum Tart

- 1 cup hazelnuts
- ¼ cup firmly packed light brown sugar
- 1 cup all-purpose flour
- ⅓ cup FILIPPO BERIO® Extra Light Olive Oil
- 1 egg, separated
- Pinch salt
- 3 tablespoons granulated sugar
- 2 teaspoons cornstarch
- ½ teaspoon grated lime peel
- Pinch ground nutmeg
- Pinch ground cloves
- 1¼ pounds plums (about 5 large), cut into halves and pitted
- 3 tablespoons currant jelly
- Sweetened whipped cream (optional)

Preheat oven to 375°F. Grease 9-inch tart pan with removable bottom with olive oil.

Place hazelnuts in food processor; process until coarsely chopped. Remove ¼ cup for garnish; set aside. Add brown sugar to food processor; process until nuts are finely ground. Add flour, olive oil, egg yolk and salt; process until combined. (Mixture will be crumbly.)

Spoon mixture into prepared pan. Press firmly in even layer on bottom and up side. Brush inside of crust with egg white. Place in freezer 10 minutes.

In large bowl, combine granulated sugar, cornstarch, lime peel, nutmeg and cloves. Cut each plum half into four wedges. Add to sugar mixture; toss until combined. Arrange plums in overlapping circles in crust; spoon any remaining sugar mixture over plums. Place tart on baking sheet.

Bake 45 to 50 minutes or until fruit is tender and juices are thickened. Cool 30 minutes on wire rack. Place currant jelly in small saucepan; heat over low heat, stirring frequently, until melted. Brush over plums; sprinkle with reserved hazelnuts. Serve tart warm or at room temperature with whipped cream, if desired.

MAKES 6 SERVINGS

Pumpkin Cake
with Creamy Orange Glaze

Cake

- 2 cups all-purpose flour
- 2 teaspoons baking powder
- 2 teaspoons ground cinnamon
- 1 teaspoon baking soda
- 1 teaspoon salt
- 1 teaspoon ground ginger
- 1 teaspoon ground nutmeg
- 1 can (15 ounces) solid-pack pumpkin
- 3 eggs
- ¾ cup packed brown sugar
- ½ cup granulated sugar
- ½ cup natural or unsweetened applesauce
- 2 tablespoons vegetable oil

Glaze

- 2 ounces light cream cheese, softened
- ¼ cup powdered sugar
- 2 to 4 tablespoons milk
- ¼ teaspoon orange extract

1. Preheat the oven to 350°F. Spray 13×9-inch baking pan with nonstick cooking spray.

2. Combine flour, baking powder, cinnamon, baking soda, salt, ginger and nutmeg in medium bowl; mix well. Stir pumpkin, eggs, brown sugar, granulated sugar, applesauce and oil in large bowl until smooth and well blended. Gradually stir in flour mixture until smooth and well blended. Pour into prepared pan.

3. Bake 30 to 35 minutes or until a toothpick inserted in the center comes out clean. Cool completely in pan on wire rack.

4. Beat cream cheese in medium bowl until smooth. Add powdered sugar; beat until well blended. Add 2 tablespoons milk and orange extract; beat until smooth. Add additional milk, 1 teaspoon at a time, until desired consistency is reached.

5. Spread glaze over cake. Let stand until set.

MAKES 24 SERVINGS

Pumpkin Cake with Creamy Orange Glaze

Peppermint Ice Cream Pie

4 cups vanilla ice cream

6 peppermint candies

1 (6-ounce) graham cracker pie crust

¼ cup chocolate syrup

Additional crushed peppermint candies (optional)

1. Scoop ice cream into medium bowl; let stand at room temperature 5 minutes or until softened, stirring occasionally.

2. Place 6 candies in heavy-duty resealable food storage bag; coarsely crush with rolling pin or meat mallet. Stir candy into ice cream; spread evenly in pie crust.

3. Cover and freeze at least 4 hours or overnight. Using sharp knife that has been dipped in warm water, cut pie into 12 slices. Transfer to serving plates; drizzle with chocolate syrup. Garnish with additional candies.

MAKES 12 SERVINGS

Cranberry Apple Pie
with Soft Gingersnap Crust

20 gingersnaps

1½ tablespoons margarine

2 McIntosh apples

1 cup fresh cranberries

5 tablespoons dark brown sugar

¼ teaspoon ground cinnamon

¼ teaspoon vanilla

1 teaspoon granulated sugar

Preheat oven to 375°F. Combine gingersnaps and margarine in food processor; process until well combined. Press gingersnap mixture into 8-inch pie plate. Press on crust with slightly smaller pie plate to make crust even. Bake 5 to 8 minutes; remove crust from oven and let cool. Slice apples in food processor. Add cranberries, brown sugar, cinnamon and vanilla; stir just until well mixed. Spoon mixture into separate pie plate or casserole dish; sprinkle with granulated sugar. Bake 35 minutes or until tender. Spoon over gingersnap crust and serve immediately.

MAKES 8 SERVINGS

Favorite recipe from **The Sugar Association, Inc.**

Peppermint Ice Cream Pie

Mini Pumpkin Pie Tarts

¾ cup plus ⅓ cup thawed frozen whipped topping, divided
½ cup canned solid-pack pumpkin
¼ cup sugar
2 ounces cream cheese, softened
1 teaspoon vanilla
¾ teaspoon pumpkin pie spice
60 mini phyllo shells, thawed
60 pecan halves (about 3 ounces), toasted*

To toast pecans, spread in single layer in heavy-bottomed skillet. Cook over medium heat 1 to 2 minutes, stirring frequently, until nuts are lightly browned. Remove from skillet immediately. Cool before using.

1. Beat ¾ cup whipped topping, pumpkin, sugar, cream cheese, vanilla and pumpkin pie spice in large bowl with electric mixer at medium-high speed until smooth and well blended.

2. Spoon 1½ teaspoons pumpkin mixture into each phyllo shell. Top with ½ teaspoon whipped topping and 1 pecan half. Cover; refrigerate at least 1 hour before serving.

MAKES 60 MINI TARTS (2 MINI TARTS PER SERVING)

Apple Custard Pie

½ cup sugar
¼ cup ARGO® or KINGSFORD'S® Corn Starch
3 eggs
½ cup margarine or butter, melted
½ cup KARO® Light or Dark Corn Syrup
1 teaspoon vanilla extract
2 large apples, peeled and thinly sliced
1 unbaked (9-inch) pie crust
2 tablespoons chopped walnuts (optional)

In medium bowl, combine sugar and corn starch. Whisk in eggs. Stir in margarine, corn syrup and vanilla extract. Fold in half of the apples. Pour into pie crust.

Place remaining apples in overlapping circle on top of pie. Sprinkle with walnuts.

Bake in 375°F oven 50 minutes or until center of pie is set. Cool on wire rack.

MAKES 8 SERVINGS

Mini Pumpkin Pie Tarts

Chocolate Chip Holiday Tea Cakes

- 1 cup (2 sticks) butter, softened
- ½ cup sifted powdered sugar
- 1 teaspoon vanilla extract
- 2 cups all-purpose flour
- ⅔ cup finely chopped nuts
- 2 cups (12-ounce package) NESTLÉ® TOLL HOUSE® Semi-Sweet Chocolate Morsels, *divided*

PREHEAT oven to 350°F.

BEAT butter and powdered sugar in large mixer bowl until creamy. Beat in vanilla extract. Gradually beat in flour and nuts. Stir in *1 ½ cups* morsels. Roll dough into 1-inch balls; place on ungreased baking sheets.

BAKE for 10 to 12 minutes or until set and light golden brown on bottom. Cool for 2 minutes on baking sheets; remove to wire racks to cool completely.

MICROWAVE *remaining* morsels in heavy-duty plastic bag on HIGH (100%) power for 30 to 45 seconds; knead. Microwave at additional 10- to 20-second intervals, kneading until smooth. Cut tiny corner from bag; squeeze to drizzle over cookies. Refrigerate cookies for about 5 minutes or until chocolate is set. Store at room temperature in airtight containers.

MAKES 54 COOKIES

Variation: For a spicier cookie, add 2 to 2 ½ teaspoons ground cinnamon to flour before adding to butter-sugar mixture.

Ribbon of Cherry Cheesecake

1 cup sliced almonds, toasted and finely chopped

1 cup graham cracker crumbs

⅓ cup butter or margarine, melted

1 (21-ounce) can cherry pie filling

¾ cup plus 2 tablespoons sugar, divided

2 tablespoons cornstarch

½ teaspoon almond extract

4 (8-ounce each) packages cream cheese, softened

3 tablespoons amaretto liqueur

1 tablespoon lemon juice

1 teaspoon vanilla extract

3 eggs, lightly beaten

Combine almonds, graham cracker crumbs and butter in medium bowl; mix well. Press crumb mixture evenly over the bottom and 2 inches up side of 10-inch springform pan. Set aside.

Purée cherry pie filling in blender or food processor until smooth; pour into medium saucepan. Combine 2 tablespoons sugar and cornstarch; stir into cherry filling. Cook, stirring constantly, over low heat until mixture is thick and bubbly. Remove from heat. Stir in almond extract. Set aside to cool.

Combine cream cheese, remaining ¾ cup sugar, amaretto, lemon juice and vanilla in large mixing bowl. Beat with electric mixer on medium speed 3 to 4 minutes, or until well mixed. Add eggs all at once; beat on low speed just until mixed.

To assemble cheesecake, pour one-third of the cream cheese mixture into prepared crust. Top with about ⅓ cup cherry purée. Swirl cherry mixture into cream cheese mixture, using knife or spatula. Repeat layers twice, ending with cherry purée. Reserve remaining purée.

Bake in preheated 350°F oven 60 to 65 minutes, or until center appears nearly set when gently shaken. Cool on wire rack. Refrigerate until ready to serve. To serve, spoon generous tablespoons of purée on serving plate. Place cheesecake wedge on top of purée.

MAKES 16 SERVINGS

Favorite Recipe from
Cherry Marketing Institute

Cranberry Apple Nut Pie

Rich Pie Pastry (recipe follows)

- 1 cup sugar
- 3 tablespoons all-purpose flour
- ¼ teaspoon salt
- 4 cups sliced peeled tart apples (4 large apples)
- 2 cups fresh cranberries
- ½ cup golden raisins
- ½ cup coarsely chopped pecans
- 1 tablespoon grated lemon peel
- 2 tablespoons butter, cubed
- 1 egg, beaten

1. Preheat oven to 425°F.

2. Prepare Rich Pie Pastry. Roll out one disc pastry into 11-inch circle on floured surface. Line 9-inch pie plate with pastry.

3. Combine sugar, flour and salt in large bowl. Stir in apples, cranberries, raisins, pecans and lemon peel; toss well. Transfer to crust; dot with butter.

4. Roll remaining half of pie pastry on lightly floured surface to form 11-inch circle. Place over filling. Trim and seal edge; flute. Reroll scraps and cut into decorative shapes. Moisten pastry cutouts and adhere to top crust as desired. Cut three slits in center of top crust. Lightly brush top crust with egg.

5. Bake 35 minutes or until apples are tender when pierced with fork and pastry is golden brown. Cool 15 minutes on wire rack. Serve warm or cool completely.

MAKES 8 SERVINGS

Rich Pie Pastry

- 2 cups all-purpose flour
- ¼ teaspoon salt
- 6 tablespoons cold butter
- 6 tablespoons shortening or lard
- 6 to 8 tablespoons cold water

Combine flour and salt in medium bowl. Cut in butter and shortening with pastry blender or two knives until mixture resembles coarse crumbs. Sprinkle water, 1 tablespoon at a time, over flour mixture, mixing until dough forms. Divide dough in half. Form each half into disc; wrap in plastic wrap. Refrigerate 30 minutes.

MAKES PASTRY FOR 1 (9-INCH) DOUBLE PIE CRUST

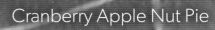

Cranberry Apple Nut Pie

Chocolate Mousse Cake Roll

Chocolate Mousse Filling (page 299)

¼ cup powdered sugar

4 eggs, separated

½ cup plus ⅓ cup granulated sugar, divided

1 teaspoon vanilla extract

½ cup all-purpose flour

⅓ cup HERSHEY'S® Cocoa

½ teaspoon baking powder

¼ teaspoon baking soda

⅛ teaspoon salt

⅓ cup water

Additional powdered sugar

HERSHEY'S® Syrup

1. Prepare Chocolate Mousse Filling. Chill 6 to 8 hours or overnight.

2. Prepare cake.* Heat oven to 375°F. Line 15½×10½×1-inch jelly-roll pan with foil; generously grease foil. Sprinkle linen or thin cotton towel with ¼ cup powdered sugar.

3. Beat egg whites in large bowl until soft peaks form; gradually add ½ cup granulated sugar, beating until stiff peaks form. Beat egg yolks and vanilla in medium bowl on medium speed of mixer 3 minutes. Gradually add remaining ⅓ cup granulated sugar; continue beating 2 additional minutes.

4. Stir together flour, cocoa, baking powder, baking soda and salt; add to egg yolk mixture alternately with water, beating on low speed just until batter is smooth. Gradually fold chocolate mixture into beaten egg whites until well blended. Spread batter evenly in prepared pan.

5. Bake 12 to 15 minutes or until top springs back when touched lightly in center. Immediately loosen cake from edges of pan; invert onto prepared towel. Carefully peel off foil. Immediately roll cake and towel together starting from narrow end; place on wire rack to cool completely.

6. Carefully unroll cake; remove towel. Gently stir Filling until of spreading consistency. Spread cake with Chocolate Mousse Filling; reroll cake. Refrigerate several hours. Sift powdered sugar over top just before serving. Serve drizzled with syrup and garnished as desired. Cover; refrigerate any leftover cake roll.

*Cake may be prepared up to 2 days in advance. Keep cake rolled tightly and covered well so that it doesn't get dry.

MAKES 8 TO 10 SERVINGS

Chocolate Mousse Filling

¼ cup sugar

1 teaspoon unflavored gelatin

½ cup milk

1 cup HERSHEY'S® SPECIAL DARK® Chocolate Chips or HERSHEY'S® Semi-Sweet Chocolate Chips

2 teaspoons vanilla extract

1 cup (½ pint) cold whipping cream

1. Stir together sugar and gelatin in small saucepan; stir in milk. Let stand 2 minutes to soften gelatin. Cook over medium heat, stirring constantly, until mixture just begins to boil.

2. Remove from heat. Immediately add chocolate chips; stir until melted. Stir in vanilla; cool to room temperature.

3. Beat whipping cream in small bowl until stiff. Gradually add chocolate mixture, folding gently just until blended. Cover; refrigerate until ready to use.

MAKES ABOUT 3 CUPS

Apple-Cranberry Tart

1⅓ cups all-purpose flour

¾ cup plus 1 tablespoon sugar, divided

¼ teaspoon salt

2 tablespoons shortening

2 tablespoons butter

4 to 5 tablespoons ice water

½ cup boiling water

⅓ cup dried cranberries

1 teaspoon ground cinnamon

2 tablespoons cornstarch

4 medium baking apples

Vanilla frozen yogurt (optional)

1. Combine flour, 1 tablespoon sugar and salt in medium bowl. Cut in shortening and butter with pastry blender or two knives until mixture forms coarse crumbs. Mix in ice water, 1 tablespoon at a time, until mixture comes together and forms soft dough. Wrap in plastic wrap. Refrigerate 30 minutes.

2. Combine boiling water and cranberries in small bowl. Let stand 20 minutes or until softened.

3. Preheat oven to 425°F. Roll out dough on floured surface to ⅛-inch thickness. Cut into 11-inch circle. (Reserve any leftover dough scraps for decorating top of tart.) Ease dough into 10-inch tart pan with removable bottom, leaving ¼-inch dough above rim of pan. Prick bottom and sides of dough with tines of fork; bake 12 minutes or until dough begins to brown. Cool on wire rack. *Reduce oven temperature to 375°F.*

4. Combine remaining ¾ cup sugar and cinnamon in large bowl; mix well. Reserve 1 teaspoon mixture. Add cornstarch to bowl. Peel, core and thinly slice apples, adding pieces after sliced; toss well. Drain cranberries; add to apple mixture and toss well.

5. Arrange apple mixture attractively over dough. Sprinkle reserved 1 teaspoon sugar mixture evenly over top of tart. Place tart on baking sheet; bake 30 to 35 minutes or until apples are tender and crust is golden brown. Cool on wire rack. Remove side of pan; place tart on serving plate. Serve warm or at room temperature with yogurt, if desired.

MAKES 8 SERVINGS

Apple-Cranberry Tart

Hidden Pumpkin Pies

1½ cups solid-pack pumpkin

1 cup evaporated milk

2 eggs

¼ cup sugar

1¼ teaspoons vanilla, divided

1 teaspoon pumpkin pie spice*

3 egg whites

¼ teaspoon cream of tartar

⅓ cup honey

*Or substitute ½ teaspoon ground cinnamon, ¼ teaspoon ground ginger and ⅛ teaspoon each ground allspice and ground nutmeg.

1. Preheat oven to 350°F.

2. Combine pumpkin, evaporated milk, eggs, sugar, 1 teaspoon vanilla and pumpkin pie spice in large bowl; mix well. Pour into six 6-ounce custard cups or soufflé dishes. Place in shallow baking dish or pan. Pour boiling water around custard cups to depth of 1 inch. Bake 25 minutes or until set.

3. Meanwhile, beat egg whites, cream of tartar and remaining ¼ teaspoon vanilla in medium bowl with electric mixer at high speed until soft peaks form. Gradually add honey, beating until stiff peaks form.

4. Spread egg white mixture over tops of hot pumpkin pies. Bake 8 to 12 minutes or until tops of pies are golden brown. Let stand 10 minutes. Serve warm.

MAKES 6 SERVINGS

Hidden Pumpkin Pies

Apple Cider Cake

Marzipan (page 305)
Red, yellow and green food colorings
1 package (about 18 ounces) spice cake mix
1¼ cups apple cider
⅓ cup vegetable oil
3 eggs
Apple Cider Filling (page 305)
Apple Cider Frosting (page 305)
2 cups coarsely chopped walnuts
Whole cloves

1. Prepare Marzipan. Divide into thirds; place each part in separate small bowl. Tint 1 bowl of marzipan with red food coloring, another bowl with yellow food coloring and remaining bowl of marzipan with green food coloring; cover and set aside.

2. Preheat oven to 350°F. Grease and flour two 9-inch round baking pans.

3. Combine cake mix, apple cider, oil and eggs in medium bowl. Beat at low speed of electric mixer until blended; beat at medium speed 2 minutes. Pour batter evenly into prepared pans.

4. Bake 30 to 35 minutes or until toothpicks inserted into centers come out clean. Let cool in pans on wire racks 10 minutes. Remove to wire racks; cool completely.

5. Prepare Apple Cider Filling and Apple Cider Frosting. Place 1 cake layer on serving plate; top with Apple Cider Filling. Top with second cake layer; frost top and side of cake with Apple Cider Frosting. Press nuts into frosting on side of cake.

6. Form red and yellow Marzipan into apple shapes. Place cloves in tops of apples for stems. Roll out green Marzipan to ¼-inch thickness; cut out leaf shapes as desired. Arrange on top and around side of cake.

MAKES 12 SERVINGS

Marzipan

1 can (8 ounces) almond paste
1 egg white
3 cups powdered sugar

Combine almond paste and egg white in small bowl. Add 2 cups powdered sugar; mix well. Knead in remaining 1 cup sugar until smooth and pliable. Wrap tightly in plastic wrap; refrigerate until ready to serve.

MAKES ABOUT 2 CUPS

Apple Cider Filling

⅓ cup sugar
3 tablespoons cornstarch
⅔ cup apple cider
½ cup apple butter
2 tablespoons lemon juice
2 tablespoons butter or margarine

Combine sugar and cornstarch in small saucepan. Stir in apple cider and apple butter; cook over medium heat, stirring constantly, until thickened. Remove from heat; stir in lemon juice and butter. Cool completely.

MAKES ABOUT 1¼ CUPS

Apple Cider Frosting

½ cup (1 stick) butter, softened
¼ cup apple cider
4 cups (about 1 pound) powdered sugar

Beat butter and apple cider in medium bowl until creamy and well blended. Gradually beat in powdered sugar until smooth.

MAKES ABOUT 4 CUPS

CAROLING
COOKIES

Gingerbread People

- ½ cup (1 stick) butter, softened
- ½ cup packed brown sugar
- ⅓ cup water
- ⅓ cup molasses
- 1 egg
- 4 cups all-purpose flour
- 2 teaspoons baking soda
- 1 teaspoon ground ginger
- ½ teaspoon ground allspice
- ½ teaspoon ground cinnamon
- ½ teaspoon ground cloves
- Assorted icings and candies

1. Beat butter and brown sugar in large bowl with electric mixer at medium speed until creamy. Add water, molasses and egg; beat until blended. Add flour, baking soda, ginger, allspice, cinnamon and cloves; beat until well blended. Shape dough into disc; wrap tightly with plastic wrap. Refrigerate 2 hours or until firm.

2. Preheat oven to 350°F. Grease cookie sheets. Roll out dough on lightly floured surface with lightly floured rolling pin to ⅛-inch thickness. Cut out shapes with cookie cutter. Place cutouts 2 inches apart on prepared cookie sheets.

3. Bake 12 to 15 minutes or until set. Cool on cookie sheets 1 minute. Remove to wire racks; cool completely. Decorate as desired. Store in airtight containers.

MAKES ABOUT 4½ DOZEN

Gingerbread People

Cobbled Fruit Bars

1½ cups apple juice

1 cup chopped dried apricots

1 cup raisins

1 package (6 ounces) dried cherries

1 teaspoon cornstarch

1 teaspoon ground cinnamon

1 package (about 18 ounces) yellow cake mix

2 cups old-fashioned oats

¾ cup (1½ sticks) butter, melted

1 egg

1. Combine apple juice, apricots, raisins, cherries, cornstarch and cinnamon in medium saucepan, stirring until cornstarch is dissolved. Bring to a boil; cook 5 minutes, stirring constantly. Cool to room temperature.

2. Preheat oven to 350°F. Line 15×10-inch jelly-roll pan with foil and spray with nonstick cooking spray.

3. Combine cake mix and oats in large bowl; stir in butter. Add egg; stir until well blended. Press three fourths of dough into bottom of prepared pan. Spread fruit mixture evenly over top. Sprinkle with remaining dough.

4. Bake 25 to 30 minutes or until lightly browned. Cool completely in pan on wire rack.

MAKES ABOUT 1 DOZEN

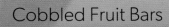
Cobbled Fruit Bars

Honey Spice Balls

½ cup (1 stick) butter, softened
½ cup packed brown sugar
1 egg
1 tablespoon honey
1 teaspoon vanilla
2 cups all-purpose flour
½ teaspoon baking powder
½ teaspoon ground cinnamon
¼ teaspoon ground nutmeg
   Quick oats

1. Preheat oven to 350°F. Grease cookie sheets. Beat butter and brown sugar in large bowl with electric mixer until creamy. Add egg, honey and vanilla; beat until light and fluffy. Stir in flour, baking powder, cinnamon and nutmeg until well blended. Shape tablespoonfuls of dough into balls; roll in oats. Place 2 inches apart on prepared cookie sheets.

2. Bake 15 to 18 minutes or until cookie tops crack slightly. Cool on cookie sheets 1 minute. Remove to wire racks; cool completely. Store in airtight container.

MAKES ABOUT 2½ DOZEN

Homemade Coconut Macaroons

3 egg whites
¼ teaspoon cream of tartar
⅛ teaspoon salt
¾ cup sugar
2¼ cups flaked coconut, toasted*
1 teaspoon vanilla

To toast coconut, spread evenly on ungreased cookie sheet. Toast in preheated 350°F oven 5 to 7 minutes, stirring occasionally until light golden brown.

1. Preheat oven to 325°F. Line cookie sheets with parchment paper or foil. Beat egg whites, cream of tartar and salt in large bowl with electric mixer until soft peaks form. Beat in sugar, 1 tablespoon at a time, until egg whites are stiff and shiny. Fold in coconut and vanilla. Drop tablespoonfuls of dough 4 inches apart onto prepared cookie sheets; spread each into 3-inch circles with back of spoon.

2. Bake 18 to 22 minutes or until golden brown. Cool 1 minute on cookie sheets. Remove to wire racks; cool completely. Store in airtight container.

MAKES ABOUT 2 DOZEN

Honey Spice Balls

Cherry Cheesecake Bars

1   can (21 ounces) cherry pie filling or topping

2   tablespoons water

1   tablespoon cornstarch

1   package (about 15 ounces) cherry chip or yellow cake mix

½   cup (1 stick) butter, melted

1   egg

1   container (about 24 ounces) refrigerated ready-to-eat cheesecake filling

1. Place cherry pie filling in medium saucepan. Stir water and cornstarch together in small bowl until cornstarch is dissolved. Stir cornstarch mixture into pie filling; cook and stir over medium heat until mixture comes to a boil. Boil 2 minutes, stirring constantly. Remove from heat; cool completely.

2. Preheat oven to 350°F. Spray 13×9-inch baking pan lightly with nonstick cooking spray.

3. Combine cake mix, butter and egg in medium bowl until well blended (mixture will be crumbly.) Press mixture into bottom of prepared pan. Bake 15 minutes. Cool completely in pan on wire rack.

4. Spread cheesecake filling evenly over crust. Spread cherry topping over cheesecake filling. Cover; refrigerate 4 to 24 hours before serving.

MAKES ABOUT 1 DOZEN

Cherry Cheesecake Bars

Buttery Almond Cutouts

1½ cups granulated sugar

1 cup (2 sticks) butter, softened

¾ cup sour cream

2 eggs

3 teaspoons almond extract, divided

1 teaspoon vanilla

4⅓ cups all-purpose flour

1 teaspoon baking powder

1 teaspoon baking soda

½ teaspoon salt

2 cups powdered sugar

2 tablespoons milk

1 tablespoon light corn syrup

Assorted food coloring, decorating gels, decorating sugars, sprinkles and decors

1. Beat granulated sugar and butter in large bowl with electric mixer at medium speed until light and fluffy. Add sour cream, eggs, 2 teaspoons almond extract and vanilla; beat until smooth. Add flour, baking powder, baking soda and salt; beat until well blended. Divide dough into four pieces; shape each piece into disc. Wrap each disc tightly with plastic wrap. Refrigerate at least 3 hours or up to three days.

2. Combine powdered sugar, milk, corn syrup and remaining 1 teaspoon almond extract in small bowl; stir until smooth. Cover; refrigerate until ready to use or up to three days.

3. Preheat oven to 375°F. Working with one disc of dough at a time, roll out on floured surface to ¼-inch thickness. Cut out shapes using 2½-inch cookie cutters. Place cutouts 2 inches apart on ungreased cookie sheets. Bake 7 to 8 minutes or until edges are set and lightly browned. Remove to wire racks; cool completely.

4. Divide powdered sugar mixture among three or four small bowls; tint each with desired food coloring. Frost and decorate cookies as desired; let stand until set.

MAKES ABOUT 3 DOZEN

Note: To freeze dough, place wrapped discs in large resealable food storage bags. Thaw at room temperature before using. Or, cut out dough, bake and cool cookies completely. Freeze unglazed cookies for up to two months. Thaw and glaze as desired.

Buttery Almond Cutouts

Buche de Noel Cookies

⅔ cup butter or margarine, softened

1 cup granulated sugar

2 eggs

2 teaspoons vanilla extract

2½ cups all-purpose flour

½ cup HERSHEY'S® Cocoa

½ teaspoon baking soda

¼ teaspoon salt

Mocha Frosting (recipe follows)

Powdered sugar (optional)

1. Beat butter and granulated sugar with electric mixer on medium speed in large bowl until well blended. Add eggs and vanilla; beat until fluffy. Stir together flour, cocoa, baking soda and salt; gradually add to butter mixture, beating until well blended. Cover; refrigerate dough 1 to 2 hours.

2. Heat oven to 350°F. Shape heaping teaspoons of dough into logs about 2½ inches long and ¾ inches in diameter; place on ungreased cookie sheet. Bake 7 to 9 minutes or until set. Cool slightly. Remove to wire rack and cool completely.

3. Frost cookies with Mocha Frosting. Using tines of fork, draw lines through frosting to imitate tree bark. Lightly dust with powdered sugar, if desired.

MAKES ABOUT 30 COOKIES

Mocha Frosting

6 tablespoons butter or margarine, softened

2⅔ cups powdered sugar

⅓ cup HERSHEY'S® Cocoa

3 to 4 tablespoons milk

2 teaspoons powdered instant espresso dissolved in 1 teaspoon hot water

1 teaspoon vanilla extract

Beat butter with electric mixer on medium speed in medium bowl until creamy. Add powdered sugar and cocoa alternately with milk, dissolved espresso and vanilla, beating to spreadable consistency.

MAKES ABOUT 1⅔ CUPS

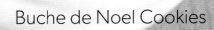
Buche de Noel Cookies

Orange-Almond Sables

1½ cups powdered sugar

1 cup (2 sticks) butter, softened

1 tablespoon finely grated orange peel

1 tablespoon almond-flavored liqueur *or* 1 teaspoon almond extract

¾ cup whole blanched almonds, toasted*

1¾ cups all-purpose flour

¼ teaspoon salt

1 egg, beaten

To toast almonds, spread in single layer on baking sheet. Bake in preheated 350°F oven 8 to 10 minutes or until golden brown, stirring frequently.

1. Preheat oven to 375°F. Beat powdered sugar and butter in large bowl with electric mixer at medium speed until light and fluffy. Beat in orange peel and liqueur.

2. Reserve 24 whole almonds. Place remaining cooled almonds in food processor. Process using on/off pulses until almonds are ground, but not pasty.

3. Combine ground almonds, flour and salt in medium bowl; stir. Gradually add to butter mixture. Beat at low speed until well blended.

4. Roll dough on lightly floured surface with lightly floured rolling pin to ¼-inch thickness. Cut dough with floured 2½-inch fluted or round cookie cutter. Place cutouts 2 inches apart on ungreased cookie sheets. Lightly brush tops of cutouts with beaten egg. Press one reserved whole almond in center of each cutout. Brush almond lightly with beaten egg.

5. Bake 10 to 12 minutes or until light golden brown. Let cookies stand on cookie sheets 1 minute. Remove cookies to wire racks; cool completely. Store tightly covered at room temperature or freeze up to three months.

MAKES ABOUT 2 DOZEN

Orange-Almond Sables

Triple Peanut Butter Oatmeal Bars

1½ cups firmly packed brown sugar

1 cup peanut butter

½ cup (1 stick) margarine or butter, softened

2 large eggs

1 teaspoon vanilla

2 cups QUAKER® Oats (quick or old fashioned, uncooked)

1 cup all-purpose flour

½ teaspoon baking soda

1 bag (8 ounces) candy-coated peanut butter pieces

½ cup chopped peanuts

1. Heat oven to 350°F. Lightly spray 13×9-inch baking pan with nonstick cooking spray.

2. Beat brown sugar, peanut butter and margarine in large bowl with electric mixer until creamy. Add eggs and vanilla; beat well. Add combined oats, flour and baking soda; mix well. Stir in peanut butter pieces. Spread dough evenly into pan. Sprinkle with peanuts, pressing in lightly with fingers.

3. Bake 35 to 40 minutes or just until center is set. Cool completely on wire rack. Cut into bars. Store tightly covered.

MAKES 32 BARS

Triple Peanut Butter Oatmeal Bars

Viennese Hazelnut Butter Thins

1   cup hazelnuts
1¼ cups all-purpose flour
¼   teaspoon salt
1¼ cups powdered sugar
1   cup (2 sticks) butter, softened
1   egg
1   teaspoon vanilla
1   cup semisweet chocolate chips

1. Preheat oven to 350°F. To remove skins from hazelnuts, spread in single layer on baking sheet. Bake 10 to 12 minutes or until toasted and skins begin to flake off; let cool slightly. Wrap hazelnuts in heavy kitchen towel; rub against towel to remove as much of the skins as possible.

2. Place hazelnuts in food processor. Process using on/off pulses until hazelnuts are ground but not pasty.

3. Combine flour and salt in small bowl. Beat powdered sugar and butter in medium bowl with electric mixer at medium speed until light and fluffy. Beat in egg and vanilla. Gradually add flour mixture. Beat in ground hazelnuts at low speed until well blended.

4. Place dough on sheet of waxed paper. (Dough will be very sticky.) Using waxed paper to hold dough, roll back and forth to form log 12 inches long and 2½ inches wide. Wrap log in plastic wrap; refrigerate until firm, at least 2 hours or up to 48 hours.

5. Preheat oven to 350°F. Cut dough into ¼-inch-thick slices; place on ungreased cookie sheets.

6. Bake 10 to 12 minutes or until edges are very lightly browned. Let cookies stand on cookie sheets 1 minute. Remove cookies to wire racks; cool completely.

7. Place chocolate chips in 2-cup glass measure. Microwave on HIGH 1 to 1½ minutes or until melted, stirring after 1 minute and at 30-second intervals after first minute.

8. Dip cookies into chocolate, coating about half of each cookie, letting excess drip back into cup. Or, spread chocolate on cookies with a narrow spatula. Transfer cookies to waxed paper; let stand at room temperature 1 hour or until set.

MAKES ABOUT 3 DOZEN

Note: To store cookies, place in airtight container between layers of waxed paper. Cookies can be frozen for up to three months.

Viennese Hazelnut Butter Thins and Kolacky (page 324)

Kolacky

(pictured on page 323)

½ cup (1 stick) butter, softened

3 ounces cream cheese, softened

1 teaspoon vanilla

1 cup all-purpose flour

⅛ teaspoon salt

¼ cup fruit spread, assorted flavors

1 egg

1 teaspoon cold water

1. Combine butter and cream cheese in large bowl; beat with electric mixer at medium speed until smooth and creamy. Beat in vanilla. Combine flour and salt in small bowl; gradually add to butter mixture, beating until mixture forms soft dough. Divide dough in half; wrap each half in plastic wrap. Refrigerate until firm.

2. Preheat oven to 375°F.

3. Roll half of dough on lightly floured pastry cloth or board to ⅛-inch thickness. Cut with 3-inch round cookie cutter. Beat egg and water in small bowl; lightly brush onto dough circles. Spoon ½ teaspoon fruit spread onto center of each dough circle. Bring three edges of dough up over fruit spread; pinch edges together to seal. Place on ungreased cookie sheets; brush with egg mixture. Repeat with remaining dough, fruit spread and egg mixture.

4. Bake 12 minutes or until golden brown. Let stand on cookie sheets 1 minute. Transfer cookies to wire racks; cool completely. Store in tightly covered container.

MAKES 2 DOZEN

Chocolate-Pecan Angels

1 cup mini semisweet chocolate chips

1 cup chopped pecans, toasted*

1 cup sifted powdered sugar

1 egg white

To toast pecans, spread in single layer on baking sheet. Bake in preheated 350°F oven 5 to 7 minutes or until lightly toasted, stirring occasionally.

1. Preheat oven to 350°F. Grease cookie sheets. Combine chocolate chips, pecans and powdered sugar in medium bowl. Add egg white; mix well. Drop by teaspoonfuls 2 inches apart onto prepared cookie sheets.

2. Bake 11 to 12 minutes or until edges are light golden brown. Let stand on cookie sheets 1 minute. Remove cookies to wire racks; cool completely.

MAKES ABOUT 3 DOZEN

Holiday Red Raspberry Chocolate Bars

2½ cups all-purpose flour

1 cup sugar

¾ cup finely chopped pecans

1 egg, beaten

1 cup (2 sticks) cold butter or margarine

1 jar (12 ounces) seedless red raspberry jam

1⅔ cups HERSHEY'S® Milk Chocolate Chips, HERSHEY'S® SPECIAL DARK® Chocolate Chips, HERSHEY'S® Semi-Sweet Chocolate Chips or HERSHEY'S® MINI KISSES®BRAND Milk Chocolates

1. Heat oven to 350°F. Grease 13×9×2-inch baking pan.

2. Stir together flour, sugar, pecans and egg in large bowl. Cut in butter with pastry blender or fork until mixture resembles coarse crumbs; set aside 1½ cups crumb mixture. Press remaining crumb mixture on bottom of prepared pan. Stir jam to soften; carefully spread over crumb mixture in pan. Sprinkle with chocolate chips. Crumble reserved crumb mixture evenly over top.

3. Bake 40 to 45 minutes or until lightly browned. Cool completely in pan on wire rack; cut into bars.

MAKES 24 BARS

Holiday Peppermint Slices

1 package (18 ounces) refrigerated sugar cookie dough
¼ teaspoon peppermint extract, divided
Red food coloring
Green food coloring

1. Remove dough from wrapper. Divide dough into thirds.

2. Combine one third of dough, ⅛ teaspoon peppermint extract and enough red food coloring to make dough desired shade of red. Knead dough until evenly tinted.

3. Repeat with second one third of dough, remaining ⅛ teaspoon peppermint extract and green food coloring.

4. Shape each portion of dough into 8-inch log. Place red log beside green log; press together slightly. Place plain log on top. Press logs together to form one tri-colored log; wrap in plastic wrap. Refrigerate 2 hours or overnight.

5. Preheat oven to 350°F. Cut log into ¼-inch-thick slices. Place 2 inches apart on ungreased cookie sheets.

6. Bake 8 to 9 minutes or until set but not browned. Cool on cookie sheets 1 minute. Remove to wire racks; cool completely.

MAKES 2½ DOZEN

Chewy Trail Mix Peanut Butter Bars

2½ cups crisp rice cereal
1¼ cups old-fashioned rolled oats
1 cup chopped mixed dried fruit (raisins, apricots, cranberries, dates and/or apples)
1 cup chopped peanuts
¾ cup SKIPPY® Creamy Peanut Butter
¾ cup firmly packed brown sugar
¾ cup light corn syrup
½ cup unsweetened cocoa powder

1. Line 13×9-inch baking pan with aluminum foil; set aside.

2. In large bowl, combine cereal, oats, dried fruit and peanuts.

3. In small saucepan, cook peanut butter, brown sugar and corn syrup over medium heat, stirring frequently, until smooth; stir in cocoa. Pour over cereal mixture; mix well.

4. Press cereal mixture evenly into pan. Let stand until set; cut into bars.

MAKES 36 BARS

Holiday Peppermint Slices

Rum Fruitcake Cookies

1 cup sugar

¾ cup shortening

3 eggs

⅓ cup orange juice

1 tablespoon rum extract

3 cups all-purpose flour

2 teaspoons baking powder

1 teaspoon baking soda

1 teaspoon salt

2 cups (8 ounces) chopped candied mixed fruit

1 cup nuts, coarsely chopped

1 cup raisins

1. Preheat oven to 375°F. Lightly grease cookie sheets.

2. Beat sugar and shortening in large bowl with electric mixer at medium speed until fluffy. Add eggs, orange juice and rum extract; beat 2 minutes. Combine flour, baking powder, baking soda and salt in medium bowl. Add candied fruit, nuts and raisins. Stir into shortening mixture. Drop dough by rounded teaspoonfuls 2 inches apart onto prepared cookie sheets.

3. Bake 10 to 12 minutes or until golden brown. Cool on cookie sheets 2 minutes. Remove to wire racks; cool completely.

MAKES ABOUT 6 DOZEN

Rum Fruitcake Cookies

Chocolate Cherry Cookies

  1   package (about 18 ounces) devil's food cake mix
  ¾   cup (1½ sticks) butter, softened
  2   eggs
  1   teaspoon almond extract
 24   maraschino cherries, rinsed, drained and cut into halves
  ¼   cup white chocolate chips
  1   teaspoon canola oil

1. Preheat oven to 350°F. Spray cookie sheets with nonstick cooking spray.

2. Beat cake mix, butter, eggs and almond extract in medium bowl with electric mixer at low speed until crumbly. Beat at medium speed 2 minutes or until smooth dough forms. (Dough will be very sticky.)

3. Shape dough into 1-inch balls. Place 2½ inches apart on prepared cookie sheets; flatten slightly. Place 1 cherry half in center of each cookie.

4. Bake 8 to 9 minutes or until cookies are no longer shiny and tops begin to crack. Cool on cookie sheets 2 minutes. Remove to wire racks; cool completely.

5. Place white chocolate chips and oil in small microwavable bowl. Microwave on HIGH 30 seconds. Repeat, stirring at 30-second intervals, until chocolate is melted and mixture is smooth. Drizzle over cookies. Let stand until set.

MAKES ABOUT 4 DOZEN

Chocolate Cherry Cookies

Cranberry Coconut Bars

Filling

- 1½ cups sweetened dried cranberries or cherries
- ½ cup sweetened shredded coconut
- ⅔ cup half-and-half or light cream
- 1 teaspoon vanilla

Crust

- 2 cups quick-cooking oats
- 1 cup packed dark brown sugar
- ¾ cup all-purpose flour
- ½ teaspoon baking soda
- ½ teaspoon ground cinnamon
- ½ cup (1 stick) unsalted butter, melted

1. For filling, heat cranberries, coconut and half-and-half in medium saucepan over medium heat. Cook 10 to 12 minutes, stirring occasionally until mixture boils and thickens. Remove from heat; stir in vanilla. Cool in saucepan.

2. For crust, combine oats, brown sugar, flour, baking soda and cinnamon in medium bowl; mix well. Add melted butter; stir until moist and crumbly. Firmly press about two thirds of crust mixture into bottom of ungreased 8-inch square baking pan. Refrigerate 30 to 60 minutes or until firm.

3. Preheat oven to 350°F. Spread cooled filling evenly over crust. Sprinkle remaining crust mixture over filling; press gently into filling. Bake 25 to 30 minutes or until topping is crisp and lightly browned. Cool completely in pan on wire rack. Cut into bars.

MAKES 20 BARS

tip

You can turn old-fashioned oats into quick-cooking oats by pulsing them in a food processor or blender.

Cranberry Coconut Bars

Lemon Bars

Crust

- 1 cup all-purpose flour
- ½ cup powdered sugar
- ⅓ cup ARGO® Corn Starch
- ½ cup (1 stick) butter or margarine, softened

Filling

- ¾ cup granulated sugar
- 2 eggs
- 1 tablespoon ARGO® Corn Starch
- ¼ teaspoon ARGO® Baking Powder
- 3 tablespoons lemon juice
- Additional powdered sugar for sprinkling over top

To Make Crust:

COMBINE all crust ingredients in a bowl until well mixed and crumbly. Press into bottom of ungreased 8×8-inch pan.

BAKE in a preheated 350°F oven for 15 to 20 minutes, or until edges are lightly browned.

To Make Filling:

MIX all filling ingredients with an electric mixer or wire whisk until well blended.

POUR filling over hot crust. Return to oven and continue baking for 18 to 20 minutes or until filling is just set.

COOL completely before cutting into bars. Sprinkle with powdered sugar.

MAKES 16 BARS

Best-Ever Peanut Butter-Oatmeal Cookies

 2   cups quick-cooking oats
 2   cups all-purpose flour
 1   teaspoon baking powder
 1   teaspoon baking soda
 ¼   teaspoon salt
 1   cup butter
 1   cup SKIPPY® Creamy Peanut Butter
 1   cup granulated sugar
 1   cup firmly packed brown sugar
 2   eggs
 2   teaspoons vanilla extract
 1   (12-ounce) bag semisweet chocolate chips, if desired

1. Heat oven to 350°F.

2. In small bowl, combine oats, flour, baking powder, baking soda and salt; mix well.

3. In large bowl, beat together butter and peanut butter with electric mixer on medium speed until smooth. Beat in granulated and brown sugars, then eggs and vanilla until blended. Beat in flour mixture just until blended; stir in chocolate chips.

4. On ungreased baking sheets, drop dough by rounded tablespoonfuls 2 inches apart. Bake 13 minutes or until golden. Transfer cookies to wire rack to cool completely.

MAKES 6 DOZEN

Molasses Spice Cookies

1 cup granulated sugar

¾ cup shortening

¼ cup molasses

1 egg

2 cups all-purpose flour

2 teaspoons baking soda

1 teaspoon ground ginger

1 teaspoon ground cinnamon

1 teaspoon ground cloves

¼ teaspoon salt

¼ teaspoon dry mustard

½ cup granulated brown sugar* or granulated sugar

Granulated brown sugar is brown sugar that has been processed to have a light, dry texture similar to granulated sugar. It can be found in the baking aisles of most supermarkets.

1. Preheat oven to 375°F. Grease cookie sheets.

2. Beat granulated sugar and shortening in large bowl with electric mixer at medium speed 5 minutes or until light and fluffy. Add molasses and egg; beat until blended.

3. Combine flour, baking soda, ginger, cinnamon, cloves, salt and mustard in medium bowl. Add to shortening mixture; beat just until blended.

4. Place granulated brown sugar in shallow dish. Shape dough into 1-inch balls; roll in brown sugar to coat. Place 2 inches apart on prepared cookie sheets. Bake 15 minutes or until lightly browned. Cool on cookie sheets 2 minutes. Remove to wire racks; cool completely.

MAKES ABOUT 6 DOZEN

Helpful Hint: Looking for something different to take to all your holiday gatherings? Decorate a metal tin with rubber stamps for a crafty look and fill it with Molasses Spice Cookies and an assortment of uniquely flavored teas. Perfect for a twist on your traditional hostess gift.

Molasses Spice Cookies

Autumn Apple Bars

1   package (15 ounces) refrigerated pie crusts (2 crusts)

1   cup graham cracker crumbs

8   cups tart cooking apples, peeled and sliced ¼ inch thick (about 8 to 10 medium apples)

1   cup plus 2 tablespoons granulated sugar, divided

2½   teaspoons ground cinnamon, divided

¼   teaspoon ground nutmeg

1   egg white

1   cup powdered sugar

1   to 2 tablespoons milk

½   teaspoon vanilla

1. Preheat oven to 350°F. Roll out one pie crust to 15×10-inch rectangle on lightly floured surface. Place on bottom of ungreased 15×10×1-inch jelly-roll pan.

2. Sprinkle graham cracker crumbs over top of dough; layer apple slices over crumbs. Combine 1 cup granulated sugar, 1½ teaspoons cinnamon and nutmeg in small bowl; sprinkle over apples.

3. Roll out remaining pie crust to 15×10-inch rectangle; place over apple layer. Beat egg white in small bowl until foamy; brush over top crust. Stir remaining 2 tablespoons granulated sugar and remaining 1 teaspoon cinnamon in separate small bowl; sprinkle over crust. Bake 45 minutes or until lightly browned.

4. Combine powdered sugar, 1 tablespoon milk and vanilla in small bowl. Add additional milk, if necessary until desired consistency. Drizzle over top. Cut into bars.

MAKES ABOUT 3 DOZEN

Autumn Apple Bars

Salted Caramel Popcorn Bars

PAM® Original No-Stick Cooking Spray

1 bag (76.3 g each) ORVILLE REDENBACHER'S® GOURMET® Naturals Simply Salted Microwave Popcorn

40 small pretzel twists, coarsely broken (40 twists = 1 cup broken pieces)

2 tablespoons unsalted butter

20 caramels (from 11-ounce package), unwrapped

1 tablespoon water

⅛ teaspoon salt

3 cups miniature marshmallows

¼ cup PETER PAN® Crunchy Peanut Butter

1. Spray large bowl, rubber spatula and 13×9-inch baking dish with cooking spray. Prepare popcorn according to package directions. Remove all unpopped kernels and place popped corn in large bowl. Add pretzel pieces to bowl.

2. Melt butter over medium heat in medium saucepan; add caramels, water and salt. Heat 5 minutes or until caramels melt completely, stirring occasionally. Add marshmallows and peanut butter; heat 1 to 2 minutes more, stirring until blended.

3. Pour caramel mixture over popcorn mixture. Toss with rubber spatula to coat. Press into baking dish; cool completely. Cut into 24 bars.

MAKES 24 SERVINGS

Cook's Tips: ORVILLE REDENBACHER'S® GOURMET® White Corn Popping Corn may be used in place of the microwave popcorn. Pop ½ cup kernels according to package directions. Use popped corn in recipe and increase salt to ¼ teaspoon.

Double Chocolate Crinkle Cookies

1¼ cups all-purpose flour

1 teaspoon baking powder

¼ teaspoon salt

½ cup FLEISCHMANN'S® Unsalted-stick, softened (½ cup = 1 stick)

1 cup granulated sugar

2 eggs

2 ounces unsweetened chocolate, melted, cooled

½ cup semisweet chocolate morsels

½ cup confectioners' sugar

1. Combine flour, baking powder and salt in small bowl; set aside. Beat FLEISCHMANN'S and sugar in large bowl with electric mixer on medium-high speed until light and fluffy. Add eggs, 1 at a time, beating until well blended after each addition. Gradually add flour mixture, beating on low speed after each addition until well blended. Stir in melted chocolate and chocolate morsels. Cover and chill 2 hours or until easy to handle.

2. Preheat oven to 350°F. Shape dough into 1-inch balls. Roll balls in confectioners' sugar to coat generously. Place balls 1 inch apart on an ungreased cookie sheet. Bake 10 to 12 minutes or until edges are set and tops are crackled. Transfer to a wire rack; cool completely. Store at room temperature in air-tight container.

MAKES 36 COOKIES

Cook's Tip: To keep hands from getting sticky, coat with a light dusting of confectioners' sugar before forming balls.

Elephant Ears

1 package (17¼ ounces) frozen puff pastry, thawed according to package directions
1 egg, beaten
¼ cup sugar, divided
2 squares (1 ounce each) semisweet chocolate

1. Preheat oven to 375°F. Grease cookie sheets; sprinkle lightly with water. Roll one sheet of pastry to 12×10-inch rectangle. Brush with egg; sprinkle with 1 tablespoon sugar. Tightly roll up 10-inch sides, meeting in center. Brush center with egg and seal rolls tightly together; turn over. Cut into ⅜-inch-thick slices. Place slices on prepared cookie sheets. Sprinkle with 1 tablespoon sugar. Repeat with remaining pastry, egg and sugar. Bake 16 to 18 minutes until golden brown. Remove to wire racks; cool completely.

2. Melt chocolate in small saucepan over low heat, stirring constantly. Remove from heat. Spread bottoms of cookies with chocolate. Place on wire rack, chocolate side up. Let stand until chocolate is set. Store between layers of waxed paper in airtight containers.

MAKES ABOUT 4 DOZEN

Chocolate Raspberry Thumbprints

1½ cups (3 sticks) butter, softened
1 cup granulated sugar
1 egg
1 teaspoon vanilla
3 cups all-purpose flour
¼ cup unsweetened cocoa powder
½ teaspoon salt
1 cup (6 ounces) mini semisweet chocolate chips (optional)
⅔ cup raspberry preserves
Powdered sugar (optional)

1. Preheat oven to 350°F. Grease cookie sheets.

2. Beat butter and granulated sugar in large bowl. Beat in egg and vanilla until light and fluffy. Mix in flour, cocoa and salt until well blended. Stir in mini chocolate chips, if desired.

3. Shape level tablespoonfuls of dough into balls. Place 2 inches apart on prepared cookie sheets. Make deep indentation in center of each ball with thumb.

4. Bake 12 to 15 minutes until just set. Cool on cookie sheets 2 minutes. Remove to wire racks; cool completely.

5. Fill centers with raspberry preserves and sprinkle with powdered sugar. Store between layers of waxed paper in airtight containers.

MAKES ABOUT 4½ DOZEN

Elephant Ears

Mincemeat Pastries

3½   cups all-purpose flour
¾   cup granulated sugar
½   teaspoon salt
½   cup (1 stick) butter, chilled
8   tablespoons shortening
1   cup buttermilk
1   cup mincemeat
¼   cup powdered sugar (optional)

1. Combine flour, granulated sugar and salt in large bowl; set aside.

2. Cut butter into 1-inch pieces. Add butter and shortening to flour mixture. Cut in with pastry blender or two knives until mixture resembles coarse crumbs. Drizzle buttermilk over top; toss just until mixture comes together to form ball.

3. Turn out dough onto lightly floured work surface; fold in half and flatten to about ½ inch thick. Knead about eight times. Divide dough in half; press each half into ½-inch-thick disc. Wrap in plastic wrap and refrigerate at least 30 minutes.

4. Preheat oven to 350°F. Lightly grease cookie sheets; set aside. Let dough rest at room temperature 10 minutes. Roll one dough disc into 18×12-inch rectangle on lightly floured work surface. Cut into 24 (3-inch) squares. Place heaping ½ teaspoon mincemeat in center of each square. Fold opposite corners each about two thirds of the way over filling, overlapping dough corners. Place 2 inches apart on prepared cookie sheets. Repeat with remaining dough.

5. Bake 20 minutes or until lightly browned. Remove cookies to wire racks; cool completely. Sprinkle pastries lightly with powdered sugar, if desired.

MAKES 4 DOZEN

Mincemeat Pastries

Christmas Tree Platter

1 recipe Christmas Ornament Cookie Dough (recipe follows)
2 cups sifted powdered sugar
2 tablespoons milk or lemon juice
Assorted food colorings, colored sugars and assorted small decors

1. Prepare Christmas Ornament Cookie Dough.

2. Preheat oven to 350°F. Roll half of dough to ⅛-inch thickness on lightly floured surface. Cut dough with lightly floured tree-shaped cookie cutters. Place on ungreased cookie sheets.

3. Bake 10 to 12 minutes or until edges are lightly browned. Remove to wire racks to cool completely.

4. Repeat with remaining half of dough. Reroll scraps; cut into small circles for ornaments, squares and rectangles for gift boxes and tree trunks.

5. Bake 8 to 12 minutes, depending on size of cookies, until edges are lightly browned.

6. For icing, combine sugar and milk in medium bowl. Tint most of icing green and a smaller amount red or other colors for ornaments and boxes. Spread green icing on trees. Sprinkle ornaments and boxes with colored sugars or decorate as desired. Arrange cookies on flat platter to resemble tree.

MAKES ABOUT 1 DOZEN

Tip: Use this beautiful Christmas Tree Platter cookie as your centerpiece for this holiday's family dinner. It's sure to receive lots of "oohs" and "ahs!"

Christmas Ornament Cookie Dough

2¼ cups all-purpose flour
¼ teaspoon salt
1 cup sugar
¾ cup (1½ sticks) butter, softened
1 egg
1 teaspoon vanilla
1 teaspoon almond extract

1. Combine flour and salt in medium bowl.

2. Beat sugar and butter in large bowl with electric mixer at medium speed until light and fluffy. Add egg, vanilla and almond extract; beat until well blended. Gradually add flour mixture, beating at low speed until well blended.

3. Shape dough into two discs; wrap in plastic wrap and refrigerate 30 minutes or until firm.

Peanut Butter Toffee Bars

1 cup SKIPPY® SUPER CHUNK® Peanut Butter

½ cup (1 stick) butter

¾ cup firmly packed light brown sugar

½ cup granulated sugar

1 teaspoon vanilla extract

2 large eggs

2 cups all-purpose flour

½ teaspoon salt

1 (12-ounce) bag chocolate chips, divided

1 cup toffee bar bits

1. Heat oven to 350°F. Grease 13×9-inch pan.

2. In large bowl, beat together peanut butter, butter, brown sugar, granulated sugar and vanilla 5 minutes or until thick and creamy. Beat in eggs, and then flour and salt. Stir in 1 cup chocolate chips. Spread evenly into pan.

3. Bake bars 25 minutes or until lightly browned. Cool on wire rack; immediately sprinkle with remaining chocolate chips. Let stand 5 minutes. Spread melted chocolate evenly; sprinkle with toffee bar bits. Cool completely. Cut into bars to serve.

MAKES 2 DOZEN

Peanut Butter and Jelly Thumbprint Cookies

  3   cups all-purpose flour

1½ teaspoons baking powder

  ½ teaspoon salt

  1   cup (2 sticks) butter

  ½ cup granulated sugar

  ½ cup firmly packed light brown sugar

  ½ cup SKIPPY® Creamy Peanut Butter

  1   large egg

1½ teaspoons vanilla extract

  ¼ cup grape jelly

1. In medium bowl, combine flour, baking powder and salt; mix well.

2. In large bowl, beat together butter, granulated and brown sugars and peanut butter with electric mixer 3 minutes or until light and fluffy. Beat in egg and vanilla, scraping down side of bowl occasionally. Gradually beat in flour mixture until blended. Wrap dough in plastic wrap; freeze at least 1 hour.

3. Heat oven to 425°F.

4. Shape tablespoons of dough into balls; arrange on ungreased baking sheets. With thumb or rounded ¼ teaspoon measure, make indentation in center of each cookie; fill each with ¼ teaspoon jelly.

5. Bake 5 minutes or until bottoms of cookies are lightly golden. Cool completely on wire rack.

MAKES 4 DOZEN

Peanut Butter and Jelly Thumbprint Cookies

Harvest Pumpkin Cookies

2 cups all-purpose flour

1 teaspoon baking powder

1 teaspoon ground cinnamon

½ teaspoon baking soda

½ teaspoon salt

½ teaspoon ground allspice

1 cup (2 sticks) butter, softened

1 cup sugar

1 cup solid-pack pumpkin

1 egg

1 teaspoon vanilla

1 cup chopped pecans

1 cup dried cranberries or raisins

Pecan halves (about 36)

1. Preheat oven to 375°F. Combine flour, baking powder, cinnamon, baking soda, salt and allspice in medium bowl.

2. Beat butter and sugar in large bowl with electric mixer at medium speed until light and fluffy. Beat in pumpkin, egg and vanilla. Gradually add flour mixture. Beat at low speed until well blended. Stir in chopped pecans and cranberries.

3. Drop heaping tablespoonfuls of dough 2 inches apart onto ungreased cookie sheets. Flatten slightly with back of spoon. Press 1 pecan half into center of each cookie.

4. Bake 10 to 12 minutes or until golden brown. Let cookies stand on cookie sheets 1 minute; transfer to wire racks to cool completely. Store tightly covered at room temperature or freeze up to three months.

MAKES ABOUT 3 DOZEN

Harvest Pumpkin Cookies

GIFT-GIVING CANDIES

Classic English Toffee

- 1 cup (2 sticks) unsalted butter
- 1 cup sugar
- 2 tablespoons water
- ¼ teaspoon salt
- 1 teaspoon vanilla
- 3 squares (1 ounce each) semisweet chocolate
- 3 squares (1 ounce each) bittersweet chocolate
- ½ cup chopped toasted pecans*

To toast pecans, spread in single layer in heavy skillet. Cook and stir over medium heat 1 to 2 minutes or until nuts are lightly browned, stirring frequently.

1. Line 9-inch square pan with heavy-duty foil, leaving 1-inch overhang on all sides.

2. Combine butter, sugar, water and salt in heavy large saucepan. Bring to a boil over medium heat, stirring frequently. Attach candy thermometer to side of pan. Continue boiling 20 minutes or until sugar mixture reaches hard-crack stage (305° to 310°F), stirring frequently. Watch closely after temperature reaches 290°F. Temperature will rise quickly and mixture will burn above 310°F.) Remove from heat; stir in vanilla. Immediately pour into prepared pan, spreading to edges. Cool completely.

3. Microwave chocolates in small microwavable bowl on MEDIUM (50%) 5 to 6 minutes or until melted, stirring every 2 minutes. Spread chocolate evenly over toffee. Sprinkle chocolate with pecans. Refrigerate about 35 minutes or until chocolate is set.

4. Carefully break toffee into pieces without dislodging pecans. Store in airtight container at room temperature between sheets of waxed paper.

MAKES ABOUT 1¼ POUNDS

Tip: Make your homemade gift even more special by creating a unique gift box. Decorate an unfinished papier mâché or wood box with acrylic paints, markers, stamps or fabric. Use masking tape to create stripes and stencils or stickers to make shapes. Line the box with coordinating tissue paper and wrap it with matching ribbon.

Classic English Toffee

NESTLÉ® Very Best Fudge

3 cups granulated sugar

1 can (12 fluid ounces) NESTLÉ® CARNATION® Evaporated Milk

¼ cup (½ stick) butter or margarine

½ teaspoon salt

4 cups miniature marshmallows

4 cups (24 ounces or two 12-ounce packages) NESTLÉ® TOLL HOUSE® Semi-Sweet Chocolate Morsels

1 cup chopped pecans or walnuts (optional)

2 teaspoons vanilla extract

LINE 13×9-inch baking pan or two 8-inch-square baking pans with foil.

COMBINE sugar, evaporated milk, butter and salt in 4- to 5-quart *heavy-duty* saucepan. Bring to a *full rolling boil* over medium heat, stirring constantly. Boil, stirring constantly, for 4 to 5 minutes. Remove from heat.

STIR in marshmallows, morsels, nuts and vanilla extract. Stir vigorously for 1 minute or until marshmallows are melted. Pour into prepared pan(s). Refrigerate for 2 hours or until firm. Lift from pan; remove foil. Cut into pieces. Store tightly covered in refrigerator. Makes about 4 pounds.

MAKES 48 SERVINGS

For Milk Chocolate Fudge: SUBSTITUTE *3½ cups* (23 ounces) or 2 packages (11.5 ounces *each*) NESTLÉ® TOLL HOUSE® Milk Chocolate Morsels for Semi-Sweet Chocolate Morsels.

For Butterscotch Fudge: SUBSTITUTE *3⅓ cups* (22 ounces) or 2 packages (11 ounces *each*) NESTLÉ® TOLL HOUSE® Butterscotch Flavored Morsels for Semi-Sweet Chocolate Morsels.

For Peanutty Fudge: SUBSTITUTE *3⅓ cups* (22 ounces) or 2 packages (11 ounces *each*) NESTLÉ® TOLL HOUSE® Peanut Butter & Milk Chocolate Morsels for Semi-Sweet Chocolate Morsels and *½ cup* chopped peanuts for pecans or walnuts.

NESTLÉ® Very Best Fudge

Buckeyes

½ cup SKIPPY® Creamy Peanut Butter*
¾ cup butter, softened and divided
2 cups powdered sugar
1 (6-ounce) bag semisweet chocolate chips (1 cup)

SUPER CHUNK® peanut butter can be used in place of the Creamy.

1. Line baking sheet with wax paper or parchment paper.

2. In medium bowl, combine peanut butter and ½ cup butter; beat together until blended. Gradually stir in powdered sugar.

3. On cutting board or flat surface, knead peanut butter mixture until smooth. Shape mixture into 54 (¾-inch) balls. Arrange balls on baking sheet. Refrigerate 30 minutes.

4. Meanwhile, in 1-quart saucepan, melt chocolate chips and remaining ¼ cup butter over low heat, stirring occasionally.

5. With two forks, dip balls into chocolate, covering two-thirds of each ball and leaving one side exposed to resemble buckeyes. Return to baking sheet. Refrigerate 1 hour or until firm. Store in tightly covered container in refrigerator.

MAKES ABOUT 54 BUCKEYES

Easy Orange Truffles

1 cup (6 ounces) semisweet chocolate chips
2 squares (1 ounce each) unsweetened chocolate, chopped
1½ cups powdered sugar
½ cup (1 stick) butter, softened
1 tablespoon grated orange peel
1 tablespoon orange-flavored liqueur
2 squares (1 ounce each) semisweet chocolate, grated or cocoa powder

1. Melt chocolate chips and unsweetened chocolate in heavy small saucepan over very low heat, stirring constantly; set aside.

2. Combine powdered sugar, butter, orange peel and liqueur in small bowl; beat with electric mixer until well blended. Add cooled chocolate; beat until well blended. Pour into pie pan. Refrigerate 30 minutes or until mixture is fudgy and can be shaped into balls.

3. Shape scant 1 tablespoonful of mixture into 1-inch ball. Repeat with remaining mixture. Roll balls in your palms to form uniform round shapes; place on waxed paper.

4. Sprinkle grated chocolate in shallow bowl. Roll balls in grated chocolate; place in petit four or candy cases. (If coating mixture won't stick because truffle has set, roll between your palms until outside is soft.) Store in airtight container up to three days in refrigerator or several weeks in freezer.

MAKES ABOUT 54 TRUFFLES

Buckeyes

Chocolate Caramels

- 1 cup (2 sticks) butter
- 1 cup granulated sugar
- 1 cup packed dark brown sugar
- 1 cup light corn syrup
- 1 can (14 ounces) NESTLÉ® CARNATION® Sweetened Condensed Milk
- 2 packets (1 ounce *each*) NESTLÉ® TOLL HOUSE® CHOCO BAKE® Pre-Melted Unsweetened Chocolate Flavor
- 1 teaspoon vanilla extract

LINE 8-inch-square baking pan with foil; grease.

COMBINE butter, granulated sugar, brown sugar and corn syrup in *heavy-duty,* medium saucepan. Cook over medium heat, stirring constantly, until mixture comes to a boil and butter is melted. Add sweetened condensed milk and Choco Bake. Cook over medium-low heat, stirring frequently, for 25 to 35 minutes or until mixture reaches 245°F on candy thermometer. Remove from heat; stir in vanilla extract. Immediately pour into prepared pan. Cool at room temperature.

LIFT from pan; remove foil. Cut into about ½-inch squares or size desired and wrap individually in plastic wrap, twisting ends. Store in refrigerator or at room temperature; use within 7 to 10 days.

MAKES 36 SERVINGS

Merri-Mint Truffles

- 1 package (10 ounces) mint chocolate chips
- ⅓ cup whipping cream
- ¼ cup (½ stick) butter
- 1 container (3½ ounces) chocolate sprinkles

1. Melt chocolate chips with whipping cream and butter in medium heavy saucepan over low heat, stirring occasionally. Pour into pie pan. Refrigerate 2 hours or until mixture is thickened.

2. Shape about 1 tablespoonful of mixture into 1¼-inch ball. Repeat with remaining mixture. Roll balls to form uniform round shapes; place on waxed paper.

3. Place sprinkles in shallow bowl. Roll balls in sprinkles; place in miniature paper candy cups. (If coating mixture won't stick because truffle has set, roll between your palms until outside is soft.) Store in airtight container in refrigerator up to three days or in freezer three weeks.

MAKES ABOUT 2 DOZEN

Chocolate Caramels

Peppermint Taffy

2 tablespoons butter, softened and divided
½ cup powdered sugar
2½ cups granulated sugar
½ cup water
¼ cup white vinegar
7 to 8 drops red food coloring
½ teaspoon peppermint extract

1. Grease 12-inch ceramic dish with 1 tablespoon butter. Line large baking sheet with foil; sprinkle with powdered sugar.

2. Combine granulated sugar, water, vinegar and remaining 1 tablespoon butter in large heavy saucepan. Bring to a boil, stirring frequently. Attach candy thermometer to side of pan, making sure bulb is submerged in sugar mixture but not touching bottom of pan. Continue boiling, without stirring, about 10 minutes or until sugar mixture reaches between hard-ball stage (265°F) and soft-crack stage (270°F) on candy thermometer. Remove from heat; stir in food coloring and peppermint extract.

3. Slowly pour hot sugar mixture onto prepared dish. Let stand 20 to 25 minutes or until cool enough to handle and indent made with finger holds its shape.

4. Using buttered hands, shape taffy into ball. Scrape up any remaining taffy with rubber spatula. Pull taffy between hands into thick rope about 18 inches long, turning and twisting taffy back on itself. Continue pulling taffy 10 to 15 minutes or until stiff with light color and satiny finish. (It's important to pull taffy long enough or it will be sticky.)

5. When taffy begins to hold folds of rope shape and develops ridges, begin pulling 1-inch-wide ropes from taffy and let ropes fall onto prepared baking sheet. Using buttered sheers, cut taffy ropes into 1-inch pieces. Cool completely.

6. Wrap taffy pieces in waxed paper. Store in airtight container at room temperature up to one week.

MAKES ABOUT 1 POUND

Lemon Taffy: Substitute 4 to 5 drops yellow food coloring for red food coloring and lemon extract for peppermint extract. Proceed as directed.

Peppermint Taffy

Fudge Rum Balls

1   package DUNCAN HINES® Moist Deluxe® Butter Recipe Fudge Cake Mix
2   cups sifted confectioners' sugar
1   cup finely chopped pecans or walnuts
¼   cup unsweetened cocoa powder
1   tablespoon rum extract
     Pecans or walnuts, finely chopped

1. Preheat oven to 375°F. Grease and flour 13×9×2-inch pan.

2. Prepare, bake and cool cake following package directions for basic recipe.

3. Crumble cake into large bowl. Stir with fork until crumbs are fine and uniform in size. Add confectioners' sugar, 1 cup nuts, cocoa and rum extract. Stir until well blended.

4. Shape heaping tablespoonfuls of mixture into balls. Garnish by rolling balls in finely chopped nuts. Press firmly to adhere nuts.

MAKES 6 DOZEN

Tip: Substitute rum for rum extract.

White Chocolate Triangles

1   cup white chocolate chips
½   cup sweetened condensed milk
½   cup chopped pecans, toasted*
½   (9-ounce) package chocolate wafers, crushed

*To toast pecans, spread in single layer in heavy skillet. Cook and stir over medium heat 1 to 2 minutes or until nuts are lightly browned, stirring frequently.

1. Grease 8-inch square baking pan.

2. Combine white chocolate chips and condensed milk in medium saucepan; cook and stir over low heat until chips are melted. Stir in pecans and crushed wafers.

3. Spread mixture in prepared pan; let stand until set. Cut into triangles and store tightly covered in refrigerator. Serve chilled or at room temperature.

MAKES 72 TRIANGLES

Fudge Rum Balls

Little Christmas Puddings

1 can (14 ounces) sweetened condensed milk
1 ounce semisweet chocolate
2 teaspoons vanilla
2¼ cups chocolate sandwich cookie crumbs
⅓ cup white chocolate chips
Green leaf sprinkles
Small red candies

1. Combine sweetened condensed milk and semisweet chocolate in medium saucepan; cook and stir over low heat until chocolate is melted and mixture is smooth. Remove from heat; stir in vanilla.

2. Stir cookie crumbs into chocolate mixture until well blended. Cover and refrigerate 1 hour.

3. Line large baking sheet with waxed paper. Shape heaping teaspoonfuls of chocolate mixture into 1-inch balls. Place on prepared baking sheet. Refrigerate until firm.

4. Place balls in 1¾-inch paper or foil baking cups on large baking sheets. Place white chocolate chips in small microwavable bowl. Microwave on MEDIUM (50%) 1 minute or until melted, stirring after 30 seconds. Spoon melted white chocolate over tops of balls. Top with sprinkles and red candies. Let stand until set. Store covered in refrigerator.

MAKES ABOUT 3½ DOZEN

Peanut Butter White Chocolate Fudge

1 (12-ounce) package white chocolate chips
1 cup SKIPPY® Creamy Peanut Butter
1 cup coarsely chopped walnuts, toasted, if desired
Melted chocolate, if desired

1. Line 8×8- or 9×9-inch pan with aluminum foil; coat with cooking spray.

2. In 2-quart microwave-safe bowl, microwave white chocolate chips and peanut butter on HIGH (100%) 1 minute or until melted; stir until smooth. Stir in walnuts. Spread into pan.

3. Refrigerate fudge 2 hours or until firm. Cut into 1-inch squares; drizzle with melted chocolate.

MAKES 64 PIECES

Little Christmas Puddings

Jingle Bells Chocolate Pretzels

1 cup HERSHEY'S® SPECIAL DARK® Chocolate Chips or HERSHEY'S® Semi-Sweet Chocolate Chips

1 cup HERSHEY'S® Premier White Chips, divided

1 tablespoon plus ½ teaspoon shortening (do not use butter, margarine, spread or oil), divided

About 24 salted or unsalted pretzels (3×2 inches)

1. Cover tray or cookie sheet with wax paper.

2. Place chocolate chips, ⅔ cup white chips and 1 tablespoon shortening in medium microwave-safe bowl. Microwave at MEDIUM (50%) 1 minute; stir. Microwave at MEDIUM an additional 1 to 2 minutes, stirring every 30 seconds, until chips are melted when stirred.

3. Using fork, dip each pretzel into chocolate mixture; tap fork on side of bowl to remove excess chocolate. Place coated pretzels on prepared tray.

4. Place remaining ⅓ cup white chips and remaining ½ teaspoon shortening in small microwave-safe bowl. Microwave at MEDIUM 15 to 30 seconds or until chips are melted when stirred. Using tines of fork, drizzle chip mixture across pretzels. Refrigerate until coating is set. Store in airtight container in cool, dry place.

MAKES ABOUT 24 PRETZELS

White Dipped Pretzels: Cover tray with wax paper. Place 2 cups (12-ounce package) HERSHEY'S® Premier White Chips and 2 tablespoons shortening (do not use butter, margarine, spread or oil) in medium microwave-safe bowl. Microwave at MEDIUM 1 to 2 minutes or until chips are melted when stirred. Dip pretzels as directed above. Place ¼ cup HERSHEY'S® SPECIAL DARK® Chocolate Chips or HERSHEY'S® Semi-Sweet Chocolate Chips and ¼ teaspoon shortening (do not use butter, margarine, spread or oil) in small microwave-safe bowl. Microwave at MEDIUM 30 seconds to 1 minute or until chips are melted when stirred. Drizzle melted chocolate across pretzels, using tines of fork. Refrigerate and store as directed above.

Citrus Candied Nuts

1	egg white
1½	cups whole almonds
1½	cups pecan halves
1	cup powdered sugar
2	tablespoons lemon juice
2	teaspoons grated orange peel
1	teaspoon grated lemon peel
⅛	teaspoon ground nutmeg

1. Preheat oven to 300°F. Grease 15×10×1-inch jelly-roll pan.

2. Beat egg white in medium bowl with electric mixer at high speed until soft peaks form. Add almonds and pecans; stir until well coated. Stir in powdered sugar, lemon juice, orange peel, lemon peel and nutmeg until evenly coated. Spread nuts in single layer in prepared pan.

3. Bake 30 minutes, stirring after 20 minutes. Turn off heat. Let nuts stand in oven 15 minutes. Remove nuts from pan to sheet of foil. Cool completely. Store in airtight container up to two weeks.

MAKES ABOUT 3 CUPS

Candy Cane Fudge

½ cup light corn syrup
½ cup whipping cream
3 cups semisweet chocolate chips
1½ cups powdered sugar, sifted
1¼ cups crushed candy canes, divided
1½ teaspoons vanilla

1. Line 8-inch baking pan with foil, leaving 1-inch overhang on sides.

2. Bring corn syrup and cream to a boil in 2-quart saucepan over medium heat. Boil 1 minute. Remove from heat. Add chocolate chips; stir constantly until chips are melted. Stir in powdered sugar, 1 cup candy canes and vanilla. Pour into prepared pan. Sprinkle with remaining ¼ cup candy canes. Cover and refrigerate 2 hours or until firm.

3. Lift fudge out of pan using foil. Place on cutting board; remove foil. Cut into 1-inch squares. Store in airtight container.

MAKES ABOUT 2 POUNDS

Glazed Almonds

1 cup blanched whole almonds (about 5 ounces)
⅓ cup water
1 tablespoon corn syrup
1 cup sugar

1. Spread almonds in microwavable pie pan. Microwave on HIGH 3 minutes, stirring after every minute. Almonds should be lightly toasted.

2. Butter baking sheet; set aside. Lightly butter side of microwavable 2-quart dish.

3. Combine water, corn syrup and sugar in prepared 2-quart dish. Microwave on HIGH 2 minutes; stir. Microwave on HIGH 5 minutes.

4. Using fork, dip almonds in syrup. Remove excess syrup by scraping bottom of almonds across rim of dish. Place almonds on prepared baking sheet. (If syrup begins to harden, microwave on HIGH 1 minute; stir.) Cool at room temperature until set.

5. Store loosely covered at room temperature.

MAKES ABOUT 1 CUP

Candy Cane Fudge

Peanut Butter Chocolate Pretzels

1   cup semisweet chocolate chips
½   cup SKIPPY® Creamy Peanut Butter
1   bag (10 ounces) pretzel rods (about 28 pretzels)
    Chocolate sprinkles, if desired

1. In medium microwave-safe bowl, microwave chocolate chips and peanut butter on HIGH (100%), stirring occasionally, 1½ minutes or until melted and smooth.

2. Dip one end of each pretzel in peanut butter mixture; arrange on wax paper-lined baking sheets. Decorate with colored sprinkles or nonpareils, if desired. Refrigerate 15 minutes or let stand at room temperature 30 minutes or until set.

MAKES 28 SERVINGS

White Peppermint Bark

2   cups (12-ounce package) HERSHEY'S® Premier White Chips
¼   to ⅓ cup crushed peppermint candy,* divided

Amount of peppermint candy can be increased or decreased according to your own preference.

1. Line cookie sheet with wax paper.

2. Place white chips in medium microwave-safe bowl. Microwave at MEDIUM (50%) 1 minute; stir. Continue microwaving at MEDIUM in 15-second increments, stirring after each heating, until chips are melted and smooth when stirred.

3. Set aside about 1 tablespoon crushed peppermint candies; stir remaining crushed candy pieces into melted chips. Pour mixture onto prepared cookie sheet; spread to about ½-inch thickness. Gently tap cookie sheet on countertop to even out thickness of mixture. Sprinkle remaining peppermint pieces over surface. Repeat tapping cookie sheet on counter until candy is desired thickness.

4. Refrigerate about 30 minutes or until firm. Break into pieces. Store in cool, dry place.

MAKES ABOUT ¾ POUND

Peanut Butter Chocolate Pretzels

Acknowledgments

The publisher would like to thank the companies and organizations listed below for the use of their recipes and photographs in this publication.

ACH Food Companies, Inc.

The Beef Checkoff

Bob Evans®

Butterball® Turkey

California Wild Rice Advisory Board

Campbell Soup Company

Cherry Marketing Institute

ConAgra Foods, Inc.

Dole Food Company, Inc.

Duncan Hines® and Moist Deluxe® are registered trademarks of Pinnacle Foods Corp.

Filippo Berio® Olive Oil

The Hershey Company

Hormel Foods, LLC

Minnesota Cultivated Wild Rice Council

National Pork Board

Nestlé USA

Ortega®, A Division of B&G Foods North America, Inc.

The Quaker® Oatmeal Kitchens

Reckitt Benckiser LLC.

The Sugar Association, Inc.

Unilever

Washington Apple Commission

Metric Conversion Chart

VOLUME MEASUREMENTS (dry)

1/8 teaspoon = 0.5 mL
1/4 teaspoon = 1 mL
1/2 teaspoon = 2 mL
3/4 teaspoon = 4 mL
1 teaspoon = 5 mL
1 tablespoon = 15 mL
2 tablespoons = 30 mL
1/4 cup = 60 mL
1/3 cup = 75 mL
1/2 cup = 125 mL
2/3 cup = 150 mL
3/4 cup = 175 mL
1 cup = 250 mL
2 cups = 1 pint = 500 mL
3 cups = 750 mL
4 cups = 1 quart = 1 L

VOLUME MEASUREMENTS (fluid)

1 fluid ounce (2 tablespoons) = 30 mL
4 fluid ounces (1/2 cup) = 125 mL
8 fluid ounces (1 cup) = 250 mL
12 fluid ounces (1 1/2 cups) = 375 mL
16 fluid ounces (2 cups) = 500 mL

WEIGHTS (mass)

1/2 ounce = 15 g
1 ounce = 30 g
3 ounces = 90 g
4 ounces = 120 g
8 ounces = 225 g
10 ounces = 285 g
12 ounces = 360 g
16 ounces = 1 pound = 450 g

DIMENSIONS

1/16 inch = 2 mm
1/8 inch = 3 mm
1/4 inch = 6 mm
1/2 inch = 1.5 cm
3/4 inch = 2 cm
1 inch = 2.5 cm

OVEN TEMPERATURES

250°F = 120°C
275°F = 140°C
300°F = 150°C
325°F = 160°C
350°F = 180°C
375°F = 190°C
400°F = 200°C
425°F = 220°C
450°F = 230°C

BAKING PAN SIZES

Utensil	Size in Inches/Quarts	Metric Volume	Size in Centimeters
Baking or Cake Pan (square or rectangular)	8×8×2	2 L	20×20×5
	9×9×2	2.5 L	23×23×5
	12×8×2	3 L	30×20×5
	13×9×2	3.5 L	33×23×5
Loaf Pan	8×4×3	1.5 L	20×10×7
	9×5×3	2 L	23×13×7
Round Layer Cake Pan	8×1½	1.2 L	20×4
	9×1½	1.5 L	23×4
Pie Plate	8×1¼	750 mL	20×3
	9×1¼	1 L	23×3
Baking Dish or Casserole	1 quart	1 L	—
	1½ quart	1.5 L	—
	2 quart	2 L	—